AF594013

EAST COAST from KINGS CROSS

Cover: LNER 4-6-2 No 2559 *The Tetrarch* seen at Potters Bar with a Kings Cross-Leeds express in 1928.
F. R. Hebron/Rail Archive Stephenson

Below: Class 'A4' 4-6-2 No 60017 *Silver Fox* leaves Welwyn North Tunnel with a Kings Cross-Leeds train in August 1956. *R. M. Newland*

EAST COAST from KINGS CROSS

ERIC NEVE

LONDON

IAN ALLAN LTD

First published 1983

ISBN 0 7110 1212 1

Published by Ian Allan Ltd, Shepperton, Surrey; and printed by Ian Allan Printing Ltd at their works at Coombelands in Runnymede, England

Bibliography

Railway World
Trains Illustrated
Railway Observer
Journal of the Stephenson Locomotive Society
Records of R. A. H. Weight
Records of The Lemsford Locomotive Society
Locomotives of the LNER (RCTS)

Below: Class 'V2' 2-6-2 No 60897 leaves Sandy with a Kings Cross-Peterborough train on 11 May 1957.
J. A. Coiley

Contents

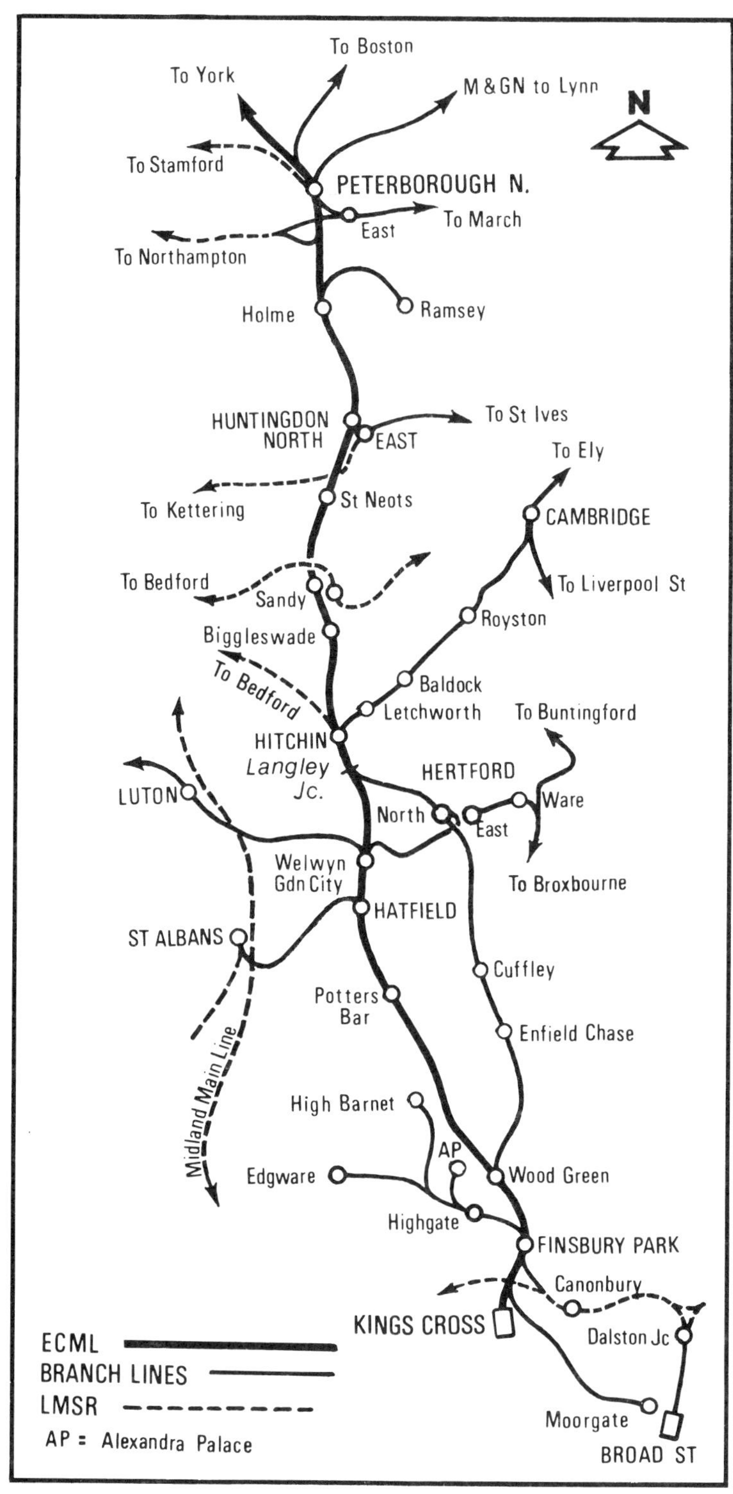

Right: The main route from Kings Cross to Peterborough in 1936.

Introduction

From its inception in 1847 the Great Northern Railway had never been fashionable amongst laymen interested in railways. For that reason it received far less attention in the railway press than the earlier trunk lines which had been established in London several years before the GNR reached the Metropolis. It has often been said the GN Locomotive Engineers 'were few and famous' — only four over 70 years, the last of whom, H. N. Gresley, went on to fame with the London & North Eastern Railway, after 1922. Similarly it may be claimed that GN enthusiasts were also few, if not so famous. Nevertheless there was much to be gained from a close interest in GN locomotives, carriages and working methods. To the select few early recorders like J. F. Vickery, K. H. Leech and above all R. A. H. Weight, those who came later owe a deep sense of gratitude. Photographers who had a liking for GN locomotives included C. Laundy, W. J. Reynolds, R. Brookman and H. G. Tidey all of whom left a notable legacy of photographs.

In August 1850 the GNR reached London from Peterborough and established a temporary terminus on the eastern side of Kings Cross goods yard close by Maiden Lane, after which the station was named. This station served until October 1852 when the permanent terminus, situated on the Old St Pancras Road, was opened. It then consisted of two large train sheds each 800ft long by 105ft wide, separated by a brick wall and covered by a double span arched roof 45ft high. Only two platforms were provided, on the eastern side for arrivals and on the west for departures, with a number of carriage roads between them. Weekday train arrivals and departures totalled 10 each. Over the next 70 years additional platforms were provided piecemeal utilising the lines originally used for carriage storage. A small extension on the western side at first served the single platform for the line from Moorgate, later enlarged to provide three suburban platforms and a small locomotive yard. In LNER days more platforms were added until the total became 16 — nine in the main line station and seven suburban (or local).

Manual signalling was controlled by two boxes, East for arrivals using platforms 1 to 5 and the up line through York Road platform used by local trains going to Moorgate, and West for departure platforms including the down Moorgate line and Milk Yard. The layout was severely restricted by the presence of Gasworks tunnel (originally Maiden Lane) only about 100yd from the platform ends.

Apart from the insertion of platforms numbered 7 and 8, in 1926 the Kings Cross terminus remained substantially unaltered throughout the period covered by this story. Compared with most other London termini it was somewhat small and lacked the grander features like Euston's Great Hall, Paddington's Lawn and the ornate Gothic exterior of nearby St Pancras. For observers the north end of the main departure platform (No 10) was the focal point affording a view of most movements within the area. Not the least interesting sight from this point was the emergence of trains from the smoke laden Hotel Curve tunnel from the Metropolitan Widened lines. Most stopped in platform 16 and on starting away with a heavily loaded eight-coach articulated set, never failed to capture interest. The engine driver would open the regulator wide while his fireman rapidly released the handbrake. Usually, after running backwards a few feet, the Gresley 'N2' 0-6-2T took hold and moved forward with an impressive beat. Only in those distressing years after World War 2 did it become possible to witness failures to start away, on any scale. On such occasions a second 'N2' had to be attached in front as far as Finsbury Park.

The locomotive yard beneath the gas holders immediately on the western side of the Gasworks tunnel, contained a turntable, small coaling plant and offices serving engines from provincial sheds being prepared for return trips and a number of suburban tank engines needing to refuel between trips. Until Nationalisation it was customary to provide a standby (pilot) engine in this yard for emergency purposes. In GN and early LNER days this was always a large Ivatt Atlantic, manned by a main line crew. The engine's steam heat valve was connected to a main running into the terminus so that empty trains could be heated while awaiting arrival of their engine. Until Gresley Pacifics became numerous a second pilot was provided at certain times of day. Usually this was an Ivatt 4-4-0 which was often called upon to assist overloaded large Atlantics out to Potters Bar or sometimes to Peterborough. This occurred far more often that the main pilot was used to replace a failed engine or one not arriving from the north in time for its booked return duty.

A now forgotten feature at Kings Cross was the minute bell, kept near the main booking hall and sounded at intervals from five minutes prior to departure of every main line train.

Leaving the terminus a northbound express plunged into the often thickly smoke laden atmosphere of Gasworks tunnel where there was a slight dip beneath the Regents Canal and a stiff 1 in 107 gradient. Emerging at Belle Isle the entrance to Kings Cross goods yard lay to the left and the North London Railway passed overhead on its lofty viaduct. In the short distance between Gasworks and Copenhagen tunnels there were once four signalboxes — Belle Isle Down, Belle Isle Up, Copenhagen Junction and Goods and Mineral Junction — the latter controlling entrance to the goods yard. Local trains for the terminus would often be held at Belle Isle Up for outgoing trains to clear. At such times one could observe shunting movements in the good yard and larger locomotives coming from 'Top Shed' for their northbound departures. Impressive sights, and sounds, of Atlantics and Pacifics on down trains emerging from the tunnel were also a never-ending source of interest to any railway minded observer.

On through Copenhagen tunnel the line rises at 1 in 110, passing beneath the flyover, carrying the goods lines, shortly after emerging at Holloway. Here the first summit was reached. On either side were carriage sidings and Clarence Yard goods to the west and East Goods on the east with views of Ashburton Grove and Highbury Vale beyond. The lines from Canonbury passed beneath before curving up to Finsbury Park station, with its 10 platforms, carriage sidings, and junctions with the branch leading to Alexandra Palace, Edgware and High Barnet climbing away on a brick arch viaduct. Just before Harringay the Tottenham & Hampstead Joint line passed beneath and the main line then continued through the extensive marshalling yards at Ferme Park and Hornsey before descending towards Wood Green (five miles). Westwards one had views of Alexandra Palace and eastwards over the Hornsey Carriage sidings Epping Forest was visible on clear days. Beyond Wood Green a flyover carried the branch to Enfield, Hertford and Langley Jct. As far as Wood Green from Holloway there was mostly six or seven running lines. At Wood Green tunnel these were reduced to four until at Greenwood Box whence only two tracks existed through the three tunnels up to Potters Bar where the 8-mile rise at 1 in 200 from Wood Green marked the summit of the climb out of the London Basin.

The line descends through Hatfield ($18\frac{3}{4}$ miles), once a busy junction serving branches to St Albans, Hertford, Luton and Dunstable and having a small engine shed housing around 28 locomotives. The four-track section from Potters Bar converged to two at Digswell crossing the 1,560ft long, 40 arch, Welwyn Viaduct 100ft above the river below. Passing through the two Welwyn tunnels a second summit was attained at Woolmer Green where four tracking resumed. Here begins a 32-mile descent to the Ouse Valley, passing Hitchin with its engine shed holding around 30 machines. Branches to Cambridge (eastwards) and Bedford (west) swung away while the main line continued into the fertile lands of Bedfordshire. There were two more short double track sections through Arlesey and Sandy. At Sandy the LNWR Oxford-Cambridge line passed over the GN and then went eastwards. Soon after St Neots the gradient is upwards through Huntingdon to a summit at Abbots Ripton. For some distance through Offord and Buckden the Great Ouse river skirts the railway, passing beneath before Huntingdon where the Midland Railway branch from Kettering came in from the west and then joined the former GN & GE Joint line at Huntingdon East station. Descending from Abbots Ripton to the level at Holme heralds a marked change in terrain as the western edge of the Fens is crossed. At Holme a single line branch trailed away eastwards to Ramsey.

Around Yaxley a further change in scenery occurs. Here extensive brick kilns with associated claypits, some being worked by dragline excavators while others have filled with water after being worked out. The acrid smell from lofty chimneys heralds the approach to Peterborough where both GE lines from the east and the River Nene are crossed by girder bridges. At Grouping and indeed until 1974 the GN station at Peterborough North consisted of two main platforms beneath an overall roof with an additional western platform and relief running lines to enable non-stopping passenger and other trains to avoid passing through the platforms. At the northern end of the down platform was a two road bay while a single bay sufficed at the south end of the up platform. Mostly the western relief platform was used by trains of the GE and LMS (Midland) section emanating at Peterborough East and for some M&GN line departures. The north bay provided a cross-platform interchange from down expresses into stopping trains to Loop line destinations and to Grantham.

From 1921 until well into BR days Peterborough North station pilot duties were carried out by Ivatt 4-4-2Ts (Class C12), besides carriage shunting and attaching/detaching odd vehicles the pilots banked down expresses when the load exceeded 40 axles (10 coaches). A smartly turned out large Ivatt Atlantic was provided as pilot at the north end, usually standing in the sidings behind the up main platform where one could often see a GE 'Claud' or even 'D13' 4-4-0 from March or Cambrdige awaiting return trains to the east.

About a mile to the north of Peterborough station, in the midst of vast marshalling yards, was New England Locomotive Depot housing some 200 engines. These worked passenger trains to Doncaster, York, Grimsby and London; fast braked goods to Colwick, Doncaster, York, Grimsby and London and every class of slow goods/empty wagons trains northwards together with the heavy coal hauls southwards to London.

Away from the bustle of London, Peterborough was always an interesting venue for the GN observers and may be instanced by the scene each weekday afternoon between 16.30 and 17.00. The 15.00 Kings Cross-Cromer arrived at 16.34 headed usually by a Pacific and Top link crew. This engine was immediately uncoupled, run forward to back on to a short train forming the 16.49 all stations to Grantham in the western relief platform. Its return working being the 'Afternoon Scotsman' from Grantham, due into London around 22.00. Standing in the north bay would be a longer rake of miscellaneous stock headed by a Doncaster Atlantic which drew its train forward and then set back on to the London train to attach the through coach for Horncastle before departing at 16.40 all stations to Doncaster via Boston and Lincoln. (After 1926 this Horncastle coach was run in the 16.00 from Kings Cross.) Next, a M&GN 4-4-0 came from Spital Bridge shed, west of the station, to take out the Cromer coaches at 16.45 for a leisurely journey via South Lynn and Melton Constable to reach their destination at 19.50. So, within the space of 15min an express had been received, divided into two parts, and three trains despatched northwards. Meanwhile the wheeltappers wielding their long-handled hammers, had tested every wheel tyre before departure — a truly Great Northern sight.

The GN London Inner Suburban district extended from Moorgate, two miles from the main terminus, on the Metropolitan Railway, to Alexandra Palace, Edgware, High Barnet, Welwyn Garden City and Hertford North. Most suburban trains used platforms Nos 12-15 at Kings Cross, but in the morning peak a number ran into the main line arrival side. Trains to Moorgate used York Road platform while those from the City emerged from the lower level into Platform 16. Until 1939 a small number of weekday departures started from Platform 17 at the back of No 16 in the Milk Dock area. All incoming trains for the local platforms 12-15 had to cross the path of trains leaving the main line station always a severe handicap to smooth working.

Finsbury Park ($2\frac{1}{2}$ miles from Kings Cross) began life in 1861 as two wooden platforms named Seven Sisters Road serving seven trains each way on weekdays. An extra down train ran Saturdays and about three each way on Sundays. In August 1869 the station was named Finsbury Park and grew to become the busiest on the GN system. In its final form there were 10 platforms, four serving up and six down trains. Broad Street (NLR) trains veered eastwards at the south of the up platforms, numbers 1 and 2, while those from the NLR passed under the main lines further south to enter Finsbury Park platforms 6-10. The High Barnet branch went up on a viaduct starting just north of those same platforms, veering westwards over heavy gradients to Highgate where the Alexandra Palace line left to reach its terminus $6\frac{3}{4}$ miles from Kings Cross. The main branch continued to Finchley (Church End — now Central) throwing off the Edgware branch westwards. This line was the genesis of the branch from Finsbury Park opened from Edgware in 1867, but latterly served by shuttle trains from Finchley only. To High Barnet (11 miles from London) the line climbed on more steep gradients to reach its terminus at the side of Barnet Hill. Both Alexandra Palace and High Barnet lines opened in 1872.

Just north of Wood Green station a fly-over rising at 1 in 55 carried the loop line through Enfield Chase (opened 1871), Cuffley (1910) and Hertford North to rejoin the main line at Langley Jct (Stevenage). From Cuffley the line was opened to goods traffic only in 1918. Passenger services to Hertford began in 1924 when a shuttle service from Baldock and Hitchin to Hertford was also introduced.

Rapid expansion of suburban passenger travel posed severe problems from 1871 onwards. To alleviate pressure on the lines between Finsbury Park, Kings Cross and Moorgate agreement was reached in 1875 between the GN Board and North London Railway whereby the latter would operate its own trains from Broad Street to certain GN suburban stations. This was facilitated by opening of a 1mile 32ch line in 1874 from Finsbury Park to Canonbury on the NLR, intended then to carry goods traffic to points in East London. By February 1875 a total of 34 weekday trains operated between Broad Street and Enfield, High Barnet and New Barnet. In June a Sunday service of 10 trains commenced, followed soon by seven more weekday trains to the newly opened Alexandra Palace terminus. Eventually Hatfield became the outermost limit of NLR operation on the main line and Cuffley on the Hertford line. Down to 1923 elderly NLR 4-4-0Ts hauled 13-coach rakes of close coupled flat roofed, four wheel stock dating from 1884. Although electrically lit, no heating was provided and third class compartments lacked upholstery to seat backs which were only shoulder high. Three other sets of LNWR origin were used occasionally. These had elliptical roofs and normal partitions between compartments. From 1933 this ancient stock was gradually replaced by bogie vehicles of Midland and LMS origin in sets of seven. Post Grouping in 1924 the LMS ran trials with a LNWR 0-6-2 'Coal Tank' No 1009 but choice of replacements for the elderly NLR 4-4-0Ts, used on the GN services, eventually fell upon LMS Standard '3F' 0-6-0Ts, popularly known as 'Jinties' and by 1929 the NL tanks had all gone. The '3Fs' remained until Broad Street services ceased in 1940, assisted from 1938 by some Stanier 2-6-2Ts on the harder turns.

By Grouping the GN inner suburban services, apart from those worked by LMS, were mainly handled by Gresley 'N2' 0-6-2Ts, condenser fitted for Moorgate running; a small number of the older Ivatt 'N1' 0-6-2Ts were also used and from time to time some standard LNER 'N7s' based on Hatfield shed. Stock by 1929 was entirely Gresley eight-coach articulated sets, known to both staff and others as 'Bogie Locals' to distinguish them from the earlier 11-coach four-wheel sets of earlier times. Forty-eight local sets then existed, 20 gas lit and the rest electrically. Tare weight varied from 144-166ton and seats for 632-648 passengers existed, divided into first, second and third classes until January 1938 when second class was abolished; first class also went in the 1940s.

In addition to local passenger traffic there was a considerable amount of transfer goods and coal from the reception sidings at Hornsey, Ferme Park and East Goods (Holloway). In the early 1930s there were 50 weekday trips via the Metropolitan Widened lines and Snow Hill to points in South London, most of which had return workings with empty wagons or goods. There were 10 trips with fish vans, horse boxes etc to Cannon Street, Clapham Junction or Victoria. Most of this work was undertaken by Hornsey shed using 'N1' 0-6-2Ts or 'J52' 0-6-0 condenser fitted saddle tanks. Kings Cross Top Shed had a small share of this work and provided an 'N1' for banking duties at Snow Hill between 10.15 and 15.30 Monday-Friday. Other transfer trips, amounting to 30 per day, went via Canonbury and Dalston to various East London points on which Hornsey used 'J52' engines. Shorter hauls from Ashburton Grove to Mill Hill, Edgware and High Barnet were covered by Kings Cros'N2s'.

As described later, diesel motive power of various kinds appeared in the late 1950s, followed in the next decade by gradual changes in traffic patterns together with reductions in schedules. To facilitate these changes much work was undertaken throughout the line of route between London and Peterborough. Firstly the notorious bottle neck at Hadley Wood was eliminated in 1959 following the construction of three new tunnels to provide four tracks between Greenwood and Potters Bar.

Early in 1972 approval was given for remodelling Peterborough North station to eliminate the 20mile/hr speed restriction caused by sharp curves at each end of the existing layout. By the end of 1969 the extensive marshalling yards at New

England had been closed as well as those formerly owned by the Midland Railway, thus facilitating provision of an extra platform to the west of the original Peterborough station and two new through fast tracks for non-stopping trains with a line speed of 100mile/h. Included in the scheme was a new power signalling installation eventually to control some 56 miles on the main line extending from Sandy to Stoke.

At the London end of the line re-signalling had been approved in 1971 to give multi-aspect signalling over the 44 miles to Sandy and associated routes worked from a new box built on the site of York Road platform at Kings Cross, to replace the box of 1932 in the middle of the yard. The scheme included a complete remodelling of the track in Kings Cross terminus and out to Holloway where a re-aligned flyover was built to take local lines over the main lines and through the existing goods tunnel to Belle Isle, thence through the western bore of Gasworks tunnel into the west side of the terminus. This work was completed in April 1977.

Electrification of the inner suburban area had proceeded from 1971 and on 8 November 1976 the GN electric suburban service was implemented. The new scheme extended from Welwyn Garden City, where a new flyover had been provided to enable electric trains to start from the existing down platform and cross the main lines without interference to fast trains, and Hertford North to Moorgate. To reach the Moorgate terminus new lines had been made from Finsbury Park to Drayton Park joining the former GN & City (Northern City) underground tracks. The final stage of electrification was inaugurated in February 1978 when outer suburban trains commenced running from Kings Cross to Royston. All locomotive hauled trains over this route were withdrawn, including the Kings Cross-Cambridge Buffet expresses. Cambridge passengers were expected to travel from Liverpool Street or change at Royston into DMUs.

Carriage sidings and servicing facilities for all electric trains were built on the site of Ferme Park yards and at Kings Cross the outer suburban trains used platforms 9-11 (formerly 11-13). The latter had been effectively segregated from the Inter City terminus by brick walls on which chalk notices appeared 'Royston Railway — Keep Out'.

For those whose interests went beyond mere recording of locomotive names, numbers and classes an attraction was the easily followed method of engine diagrams and crew rosters, also rolling stock workings. Much of this had remained unchanged from 1923-39, some even dating back well into GN times. The gradual increase in lodging away duties starting in 1923 with the London-Leeds section of the 'Harrogate Pullman', rising to a maximum of five on mid-week days between Kings Cross and Newcastle operated from either end.

Wartime conditions caused all lodging turns to be abandoned and short out and home duties similar to those in force between 1919-26 were substituted. Grantham was the furthest point reached by London crews, while Peterborough and Grantham continued working both to London and Doncaster or York. Men from Leeds, York and Newcastle were no longer seen in London. Regular observation was impossible for many reasons but a small number of people did contrive to maintain contact on a reduced scale.

Far reaching changes occurred in 1940 when working of the High Barnet line was taken over by London Transport tube trains in April. Following intensive bomb damage the 65-year old North London services between Broad Street and GN line stations was completely withdrawn in October and in 1941 the few remaining peak hour GN trains to/from Moorgate also ceased after extensive bomb damage at Moorgate station. Thus, in the space of a few months the entire complexion of GN inner suburban services changed for ever as postwar operations never reached the same levels.

When war ended a new generation of young observers arose to swell the ranks and from 1945-57 many became regular members of the lunchtime gathering at Kings Cross. By this means daily contact was maintained with events and friendly relationships established with railwaymen of all grades which enabled us to keep abreast of constant changes. New locomotive classes appeared and established favourities, notably the Ivatt Atlantics, faded from the scene. Nationalisation in 1948 brought heated, but never acrimonious, debates for and against. New liveries, rolling stock and re-introduction of intensive diagramming played havoc with accustomed procedures until the arrival of the first main line diesels in 1958. This heralded an increasing diminution of interest by older enthusiasts, one of whom aptly remarked. 'Henceforth we must take note of what occurs without trying to understand'.

1923-1930

When the erstwhile Great Northern Railway was amalgamated with the Great Central, Great Eastern, North Eastern, North British and Great North of Scotland Railways on 1 January 1923 the average enthusiast of the time had very little information about what was happening. Most matters of general interest had to be obtained by personal observation, particularly where locomotives were concerned. So far as train services were concerned things went on as before with Ivatt Atlantics hauling the majority of expresses assisted out to Potters Bar by a 4-4-0 or Gresley 'N2' 0-6-2T when the load was above about 450ton but sometimes 4-4-0 pilots went through to Peterborough or Grantham. Semi-fast and main line stopping trains

1
'Klondyke' 'C2' 4-4-2 No 3252 breasts Holloway summit with a Kings Cross-Cambridge stopping train c1925. *E. Neve collection*

had more variety in their locomotives; Atlantics, large and small; 4-4-0s and Gresley 'K2' 2-6-0s all took a regular share in those duties whilst the few Cambridge through trains had Atlantics of both varieties; Ivatt superheated 4-4-0s of Class D1 plus a few 'D2' and 'D3' on the easier turns. Through workings to and from Luton and Dunstable were in the hands of Hatfield based engines; 4-4-0s on the best jobs and Gresley 'N2s' on stopping services, but sometimes the Ivatt 'J1' 0-6-0s would appear. The heaviest braked goods, running mainly at night were being taken over by Gresley 2-6-0s of Class K3, leaving the partly braked and lighter jobs to the smaller 'K2' class. Although there were still a few Ivatt 0-8-0s ('Long Toms') at work in the district, most coal and goods trains running unbraked and loose coupled were in the hands of Gresley 2-8-0 of both two and three-cylinder varieties ('O1' or 'O2'). London suburban services were by then firmly in the hands of Gresley 'N2' 0-6-2Ts, helped out by a few Ivatt 'N1s'. A small number of Ivatt 4-4-2Ts which had seen use on the inner suburban trains down to 1921 were retained at Hatfield for use on the branches to St Albans, Hertford and Luton. Only two Gresley Pacifics were then at work, both based at Doncaster and working up to London on weekdays with Yorkshire expresses due into Kings Cross at 13.55 and 16.00 and returning at 16.00 and 17.40 respectively.

One of the first visible signs of change in ownership came on 20 February 1923 when Class J3 0-6-0 No 1170 returned to the London district from overhaul at Doncaster Plant with the letters L&NER on its tender and the number below. Hitherto GN engines had carried their numbers on the cab sides, or on bunkers of tank engines. Sub-

sequently several variations of style were seen eg 'D3' 4-4-0 with cabside number 1346 and plain tender whilst others carried LNER lettering pending a decision to standardise on 7½in shaded lettering LNER with 12in numerals below on tenders or tank sides. The livery adopted was GNR grass green with black and white edging for passenger tender and tank engines and black with red lining for all other classes. From September 1923 engine numbers began to receive suffixes; N for ex-GN; C for ex-GC E for ex-GE; D for ex-NE; B for ex-North British and S for ex-GNS. By no means all engines carried these suffixes which went out of use from February 1924 when the decision had been taken to renumber all pre-Grouping engines, except those of the North Eastern Railway which retained their original numbers. With certain exceptions, mainly duplicate engines, GN engines had 3,000 added to existing numbers, GC 5,000; GE 7,000; NB 9,000 and GNS 6,800. The small stock of ex-Hull & Barnsley engines were specially renumbered in the series 2405-2542. The earliest recorded renumbering was on 13 February 1924 when 'N2' No 4751 appeared. Although new numbers were supposed to be affixed as engines passed through works, some main sheds undertook this work. On 30 March the tanks off Stirling 0-6-0ST No 4050 were seen drying outside Hornsey shed after new numbers had been applied.

Midsummer 1923 brought the earliest signs of impending changes in locomotive power. The 10 additional Pacifics ordered by the GN in 1922 all entered service between February and September 1923 when their sheds were: Kings Cross Nos 4474/5; Grantham Nos 4476/9/80; Doncaster Nos 4472/3/7/8/81. To provide a comparison between GN and NE Pacific designs, the Darlington built Raven No 2400 *City of Newcastle* ran trials between Doncaster and London usually arriving at 13.47 with a return at 17.40 in June when Gresley Pacific No 4472 ran in opposition. Although there had been isolated cases of NE engines working into London in the years 1900/06/14, mostly with troop specials made up of Westinghouse braked stock, for which the GN had no suitably equipped engines, this was the first real use of a 'foreign' engine on timetabled trains out of Kings Cross.

Undoubtedly the greatest impact made on GN line observers was the influx of Great Central locomotives, influenced by the newly appointed Locomotive Running Superintendent W. G. P. Maclure who had occupied a similar position at Gorton for many years. To clarify subsequent events it is as well to explain that on the GN both locomotive running and engineering functions were carried out by one officer — the Locomotive Engineer. Obviously one man could not control both functions on the greatly enlarged group under which the running side was split up into areas coinciding with operating areas.

The first known appearance of a GC locomotive working GN line express trains occurred on Thursday 19 July 1923 when Class B3 4-6-0 No 1166 *Earl Haig* began a series of trials between Doncaster and London in the charge of Gorton driver Willoughby Lea. It was seen arriving at 16.00 on a West Riding express and returning with the 17.30 Newcastle diner. On both 20 and 21 July No 1166 arrived in Kings Cross at 13.55 and returned with the heavy 16.00 down. This was in furtherance of Maclure's intention to find suitable use for the six 4-6-0s built at Gorton in 1917-20 as GC Class 9P numbered 1164-9. Originally intended as replacements for 'Director' 4-4-0s (LNER 'D10/11') and the unsuccessful 'Sam Fay' 4-6-0s (LNER 'B2'), Nos 1164-9 also failed to come up to expectations and were confined to the slower Manchester-London or Cleethorpes trains until 1923.

The tractive effort of the 'B3' was about 30% greater than the superheated, piston valve variety of Ivatt Atlantics currently in use on the GN section and which were expected to work a new Pullman service commencing on 9 July 1923. Although Pullman cars had operated on the Great Northern Railway from 1879 until about 1895, mostly singly or in pairs, these privately owned vehicles were virtually unknown to lineside observers prior to 1923. One LNER constituent, the Great Eastern Railway, by virtue of ideas formulated by its American General Manager, Henry Thornton, had entered into a contract with the Pullman Car Co, in 1920 to operate a number of cars in East Englia. Experience proved, with the exception of Continental boat trains via Parkeston Quay, that such luxury travel was not desired by users of GE expresses. The LNER lost little time in finding a more suitable use for most of the Pullmans based on GE lines.

The first fruit was an all-Pullman express service operating between Kings Cross, Leeds, Harrogate and Newcastle in either direction each weekday.

Nothing was left to chance in those days so a trial trip from London to Harrogate, made up of six Pullman cars and a GN bogie brake van, went from Kings Cross on Saturday 30 June with a complement of LNER Officers and pressmen. Returning next day the overall journey from Leeds to Kings Cross took 199min. Atlantic engine numbered 1459 (GN series) was handled by its regular driver who also worked the initial trip of the 'Harrogate Pullman' down to Leeds on 9 July. The non-stop run of 185.7 miles between those points was booked in 3hr 25min, equalling the best that had ever operated, and was also the longest non-stop run on the LNER at that time. For the first month Ivatt Atlantics covered all these Pullman duties after which 'B3s' went into use.

Having successfully launched the first all-Pullman express services between Kings Cross and Newcastle via Leeds and Harrogate the previous year, the LNER decided to extend Pullman facilities to Sheffield commencing 2 June 1924. Departures were from London at 11.05 and Sheffield at 16.45 routed via the GN main line to Grantham, thence to Nottingham Victoria and the GC line to Sheffield. Northbound Nottingham was reached at 13.28 and Sheffield at 14.20. Southbound arrival at Kings Cross was at 20.00. The somewhat curious locomotive arrangements involved Kings Cross Large Atlantics taking the down train to Sheffield on Monday, Wednesday and Friday and then working a GC line train on to Manchester where the crews lodged overnight. More remarkably the opposite turns were undertaken by Gorton engines and men who worked a train to Sheffield before taking the Pullman through to Kings Cross and lodging there. It is known that Kings Cross Top Shed had difficulty in persuading sufficient men to undertake this duty but eventually recruited four sets from goods links to do so. The four drivers were: W. Sparshatt, T. Toplis, W. Payne and T. Ellis all of whom later reached the No 1 link at Top Shed although Ellis did not do so until some 12 years because his seniority was much lower than the others. Just why Gorton was selected to undertake this duty remains unclear.

The first day's trains were hauled by 'C1' No 4426 (T. Toplis) from London and from Sheffield by Class B2 No 425c *City of Manchester*. The latter no doubt influenced by W. G. P. Maclure. However, this scheme did not meet with success because after four round trips No 425c was replaced by Class B3 No 1164c *Earl Beatty*. This engine was not fit to take the 11.05 from Kings Cross on Tuesday 17 June so the Gorton crew were given one of Top Shed's best performing Atlantics No 1459. Because the Gorton drivers did not have the required route knowledge between Nottingham and Kings Cross a conductor driver was provided for that section by Grantham shed. The man who undertook that duty on 17 June related to the author how he found the Gorton fireman filling No 1459's firebox to capacity, remarking 'We shall never get out of Kings Cross unless I do'. The amazed Grantham driver said 'Put no more coal on that fire until I say'. They duly went down into the terminus, using the pricker to enliven the thick fire, and later sailed up the grades through Holloway, Potters Bar and on to Woolmer Green (24 miles) before more coal was needed! From that day on Kings Cross Atlantics undertook all the 'Sheffield Pullman' duties until 10 and 12 July when the Gorton men took down a Kings Cross based 'B3' No 1165 *Valour*. Somewhere prior to this a Sheffield 'Small Director' 4-4-0 No 437c *Prince George* brought the up Pullman into London and later caused a stir amongst the enthusiast fraternity by working some Kings Cross duties on slow or semi-fast passenger trains, making four return trips to Peterborough, and one each to Baldock and Huntingdon before it was provided to work the 18.05 Pullman on 18 July. It failed at Peterborough where 'C1' No 4407 replaced it. The 'Director' returned to London and eventually went north on 23 July hauling the 10.15 Doncaster stock train.

Loadings of the 'Sheffield Pullman' were exceedingly poor so from 14 July 1924 times were altered to give a Sheffield departure at 10.30, reaching Kings Cross at 13.45 and returning north at 18.05 to arrive Sheffield at 21.20. From that date all locomotive duties were undertaken by Kings Cross engines and men, going on to Manchester as before and lodging overnight. Balancing Sunday turns had to be provided, but regrettably full details of these are not now available.

By the autumn of 1923 the first 12 Gresley Pacifics were in service, divided between the three principal sheds: Kings Cross Nos 4474/5; Grantham Nos 4476/9/80; Doncaster Nos 4470-3/7/8/81. That over half should be concentrated at Doncaster remains a mystery, bearing in mind they had only two daily diagrams to London. So the majority of main line trains at Kings Cross were still

2
GNR 2-6-0 No 1651 heads north with a fitted goods train near Wood Green, just before Grouping.
Ian Allan Library

3
September 1922 — GNR Pacific No 1471 storms northwards past Wood Green with a 610ton test train of 20 bogies. The trial run was from Kings Cross to Grantham and return. *H. Gordon Tidey*

4
One memory of North London trains on the GN main line. 4-4-0T No 2854 makes good progress past Wood Green with a typical NLR 'birdcage' set on the 17.07 from Broad St. *F. R. Hebron/Rail Archive Stephenson*

5
High Barnet station. North London Railway 4-4-0T No 47 pauses outside the station. Note the bell on the signalbox. *E. Neve collection*

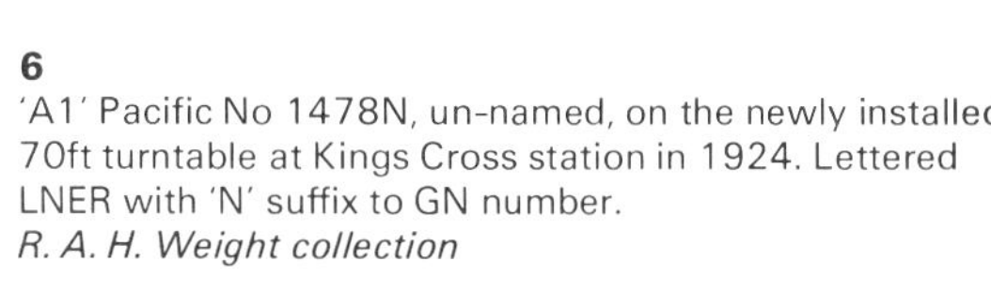

6
'A1' Pacific No 1478N, un-named, on the newly installed 70ft turntable at Kings Cross station in 1924. Lettered LNER with 'N' suffix to GN number.
R. A. H. Weight collection

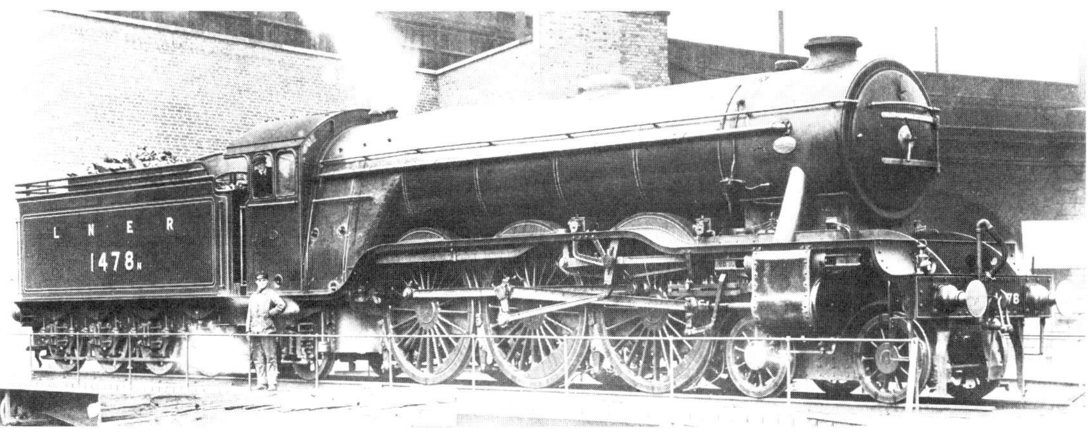

7
New Barnet, 1924. Raven Pacific No 2400 *City of York* heads the 11.30 Kings Cross-Doncaster. *F. R. Hebron/ Rail Archive Stephenson*

handled by large Atlantics whilst secondary passenger duties were in the hands of small Atlantics ('Klondykes') and Ivatt 4-4-0s. At Grouping the GN was plentifully endowed with mixed traffic 2-6-0s in the shape of 75 two-cylinder variety 'K1/2') and 10 three-cylinder 'K3' class. Between them these covered all the fast fitted goods and slower partly braked trains together with certain outer suburban passenger duties in the London district. Normally London based engines of goods trains did not go beyond Peterborough whereas those at the latter shed worked to Colwick, Grimsby, Doncaster and York. It was most noticeable at peak holiday times how the 'K2' 'Ragtimes' undertook a substantial share of hauling many additional express passenger trains.

Events of National importance staged at Wembley in 1924 made it a year notable for a greatly increased number of excursions. In April the FA Cup Final attracted six North Eastern Atlantics of Classes C6/7 plus GC B3 4-6-0 No 1169 from Grimsby. After that the British Empire Exhibition caused many special excursions to run on weekdays bringing strange locomotive classes to Kings Cross for the first time to excite the interest of observers and photographers alike. From the North Eastern Area came Atlantics of both Classes C6 (Worsdell) and C7 (Raven), plus a 'C8' Compound. Also 4-4-0s of Classes D17/20 and even a couple of 'B13' 4-6-0s — a very rare sight south of Peterborough. One of the latter, No 2009D had to be stopped for repair at Kings Cross after which it took the 7.45 slow passenger train to Peterborough whilst 'D20' No 2018D was on the 17.50 Huntingdon train on both 10 and 11 July. GC classes included 'D9' 4-4-0 in addition to 'B3' and 'B7' 4-6-0s which arrived from Grimsby frequently.

Provision of stock for the extra trains put a strain on reserves in the West Riding of Yorkshire, so two sets of Westinghouse air braked stock were borrowed from the GE section together with two 'B12' 4-6-0s to work them. So in June/July/August 1924 the two 'B12s' (Nos 1552E and 1561E) made several trips down to Kings Cross, believed to be the earliest examples of the class to work over the GN main line into London.

Spring 1924 saw the first ever Race Specials from Kings Cross to Newmarket via Hitchin and Cambridge. On 24 April Atlantic No 1427 hauled six red-liveried SECR Pullmans, *Flora, Hilda, Montana, Thistle, Albatross* and *Dora*, followed by a train of ordinary corridor stock in charge of No 1444. Such was the popularity of these trains that two weeks later the Pullman had risen to a substantial 10-car load with engine No 1460. Prior to 1924 these Newmarket specials had been operated by the GER from St Pancras, running via Kentish Town, South Tottenham and Broxbourne to Cambridge and Newmarket.

Further interest was aroused by the first appearance of Great Eastern engines from Cambridge via Hitchin. The earliest recorded was on 25 February when Class D13 4-4-0 No 1035E came up with horse boxes, followed three days later by one of the famed 'Claud Hamilton' 4-4-0s No 1835E on a special. 30 October saw 'B12' No 1536 with a GE line express diverted to Kings Cross by reason of a blockage on the normal Cambridge-Liverpool Street route. A more notable sight on 12 November was 'E4' 2-4-0 No 7501 which reached Kings Cross at 12.03 with a semi-fast from Cambridge and returned similarly at 13.45.

Another remarkable event came in the autumn of 1924 when Royal Trains between London and Wolferton were transferred from the former GE route using St Pancras (as for the Newmarket specials), to Kings Cross. A trial run from Kings Cross to Kings Lynn and back was made on 10 October using the GN Royal Train hauled by the specially embellished 'Claud Hamilton' 4-4-0 No 1873E which had travelled from Stratford via Victoria Park, Dalston Canonbury and Finsbury Park. Seven days later the same engine brought the first Royal Train into Kings Cross from Wolferton at 12.55, thus setting the pattern for the ensuing 30 years.

The initial two years of LNER ownership had produced much to keep lineside observers active but nothing so momentous as the events of April 1925 bringing the greatest excitement since the Race to Aberdeen in 1895. Press reports had told of an impending exchange of locomotives between the LNE and GW Railways whereby a GW 'Castle' 4-6-0 would operate between Kings Cross and Doncaster while a Gresley Pacific travelled between Paddington and Plymouth. The background to this story need not be recapitulated here.

A week's preliminary running commenced on 20 April when the GW 'Castle' No 4079 *Pendennis Castle* left Kings Cross at 10.12 with the stopping train to Peterborough whence return was made at

14.58 with an express from Newcastle. On the next two days No 4079 went to Grantham with the 11.30 semi-fast York train and returned thence at 16.14 on a similar train. The 10.10 Leeds express was taken to Doncaster on Thursday with a return next day at 04.24 from Doncaster.

For the tests starting on Monday 27 April No 4079 took the 10.10 as far as Grantham on Monday, Wednesday and Friday, returning from there at 15.17 with the Harrogate express. On Tuesday, Thursday and Saturday the 13.30 West Riding express was taken to Doncaster returning thence with the heavy 17.30 ex-Leeds leaving Doncaster at 16.21 and reaching Kings Cross at 21.25. The author has a faint recollection of being allowed out of school one day to see *Pendennis Castle* pass on a down run but was not old enough to understand the significance of the event. On the GWR, Pacific No 4474 (then un-named) put up a really creditable performance in the hands of Top Shed's driver Albert Pibworth. Regrettably the performance of No 2545 working on the opposite turns to No 4079 fell far below potential and for the time being laurels rested with the 'Castles'. It was fated to be 10 years before the Gresley Pacifics realised their full potential to the unbounded delight of their supporters.

Returning to other matters, Sunday 12 April 1925 saw the first booked use of pairs of large Atlantics on down expresses from Kings Cross. Hitherto it had been the practice to provide an Ivatt 4-4-0 as assisting engine when loads exceeded the single Atlantic limit. Sometimes the pilot went through to Peterborough or Grantham and was coupled inside the train engine, but often the pilot was detached at Potters Bar where a special stop was made and the assisting engine returned light to London as was always the case when an 'N2' 0-6-2T was used as pilot. The first trains noted with pairs of Atlantics on 12 April were 11.40 Newcastle loaded to 11 bogies plus a triplet Restaurant car set equalling 510ton headed by Nos 4437 and 4423, and the 12.00 West Riding with 13 bogies in charge of Nos 3288 and 3301. In each case engines went through to Peterborough.

Developments in the field of Pullman trains came in April 1925 when the ill-starred Sheffield train was re-routed, omitting Nottingham to travel via Retford to Sheffield and then extended to Manchester Central, reached at 22.12. Morning departure from Manchester was at 9.50 and arrival in London 14.00. Kings Cross engines and men continued to work these duties lodging at Trafford Park except on Saturday nights when the engine was stabled at Gorton. The balancing Sunday turns then were 12.00 Kings Cross to Retford and then from there to Manchester with GC line trains via Sheffield. From Manchester a similar arrangement applied with arrival in Kings Cross at 22.20. The Lincoln engine which hitherto had taken the GC train to Sheffield and return instead took the Leeds express from Retford to Doncaster where it remained to take over the 17.30 ex-Leeds which was worked from Retford to London by the Kings Cross Atlantic arriving from Manchester. The latter train then continued to Lincoln hauled by the engine which had been to Doncaster and back.

This Pullman service still failed to attract custom so in September 1925 it was abandoned and the cars used for a completely new service to Leeds and Bradford. It left Kings Cross at 11.10, ahead of the 'Harrogate Pullman' at 11.20 which was then altered to travel non-stop each way between London and Harrogate via Shaftholme Jct, Church Fenton and Tadcaster thus inaugurating a 198.8-mile non-stop run. These changes brought a new Leeds Pullman Link into being at Top Shed incorporating six sets of men, each booked to a regular Atlantic. The six-week roster included three lodging turns to Leeds and covered the new 'West Riding' Pullman exclusively whilst the 'Harrogate Pullman' was shared with Leeds (Copley Hill) who used 'B3' 4-6-0s at first between Harrogate and London.

Inevitably the various changes made in Pullman and Royal train workings, overshadowed less glamorous events taking place on more humble duties. Back in July 1923 when GC 4-6-0s began to appear on the GN lines, trials were also made using one of Robinson's large boilered 2-8-0s Class O5 No 17 running from Peterborough to Hornsey with coal trains and back with empty wagons. This was followed in August-November by examples of the most widely known GC heavy goods engines; 'O4' 2-8-0 and 'Q4' 0-8-0. Firstly three of the well-known 'O4' class, Nos 5391, 6289/94 appeared at Hornsey from Peterborough and then 'Q4' Nos 960/1, 5062, 5152, 6140/80. More appeared in 1925 but the class did not settle at New England where several 'O4' 2-8-0s were based from the spring of that year to operate lighter trains to Hornsey or Kings Cross goods.

8
'A1' Pacific No 4472 with LNER coat of arms on the cabsides in Kings Cross station loco yard, 1926.
F. R. Hebron/Rail Archive Stephenson

9
'D2' 4-4-0 No 1326 on Kings Cross station loco yard turntable. Note L&NER lettering. *LPC/Ian Allan Library*

10
Down Class 'A' empties train passes Greenwood behind '04' 2-8-0 No 6284 in 1925. *F. R. Hebron/ Rail Archive Stephenson*

11

An interesting working. Ex-GCR 'D10' 4-4-0 No 437C *Prince George* (with LNER on tender, but GC numberplates at Greenwood in 1924 on the 17.50 Kings Cross-Huntingdon.
F. R. Hebron/Rail Archive Stephenson

12

The Kings Cross scene in 1925. Grantham 'C1' 4-4-2 No 4401 starts the 13.40 Harrogate express from Platform 6. The West signalbox is behind the engine, East box is far left. Ivatt 'N1' 0-6-2T (in GNR livery still) as station pilot. *F. R. Hebron/Rail Archive Stephenson*

13

Great Central 'B3' 4-6-0 No 6169 *Lord Faringdon* (with LNER chimney) at Hadley Wood with the down 'Harrogate Pullman'. *Real Photos*

From mid-1924 the first production batch of LNER standard Gresley Pacifics, Class A1, numbered 2543-62 began to emerge from Doncaster works. There were not sufficient of these at work to make any great impact on the summer services but Kings Cross Pacifics then began to travel to Doncaster and return each weekday taking the 10.10 Leeds down and arriving back at 18.15.

A new dimension was introduced in the ever-present problem of operating heavy coal trains from Peterborough up to London when the first Gresley Mikado 2-8-2 No 2393, Class P1 commenced work in September 1925. This engine had a booster driving the rear carrying wheels beneath the cab which added 9,000lb of tractive effort to the 38,500lb provided by the driving wheels. It was able to haul 100 loaded wagons of coal, an increase of 20 wagons over the loads handled by 2-8-0 engines. It was joined in December by a second 'P1', No 2394. Although these experimental locomotives were capable of handling the 1,600ton trains envisaged, problems were encountered by the lack of sufficient loops to accommodate the great length. To enable the pair to work regularly between New England and Ferme Park yards a special diagram was devised. Commencing from New England each weekday morning at 9.15 the 100 wagon train was due into Ferme Park at 15.35 after lengthy stops en route to enable passenger trains to traverse the two-track sections. Return was at 5.20 next morning taking 100 empty wagons down to Peterborough. At this early hour it was possible to path the train over the fast line from Wood Green to Biggleswade where a stop was made for water, thus enabling the whole 73-mile journey to be completed in about four hours. Because of their restricted nature the two engines were not popular with the Operating Department and the frequent stopping and starting encountered on southbound journeys increased coal consumption considerably. When certain intermediate signalboxes were closed and replaced by automatic colour lights, problems increased over tight clearances so loads were reduced to 92 wagons. When the streamlined 'Silver Juibilee' train was introduced in 1935 the special diagrams were abolished and the two Mikados were used along with 'O1' and 'O2' 2-8-0s on ordinary 80 wagon trains.

Completion of the 20 Gresley 'A1' Pacifics built at Doncaster in 1924-25 was effected in July 1925. These were allocated: Doncaster Nos 2543/4/9/54/5/6/61/2; Grantham Nos 2547/8/50/1/6/7/8; Kings Cross Nos 2545/6/52/9/60. Their arrival enabled all 15 Class D1 Ivatt Superheated 4-4-0s numbered 3051-65 to be transferred to Scotland and most of their work on GN lines to be taken over by large Ivatt Atlantics displaced by the Pacifics. By this time the Pacifics had begun to receive their racehorse names, which gave added interest to the local recorders most of whom quickly adopted a particular engine as his favourite. This gave rise to a close watch being kept on all the various workings as well as getting to know the regular drivers since the time honoured practice of booking engines to crews was continued, albeit not so strictly as before.

The General Strike of 1926 wreaked havoc on all railways for a time, tending to delay further changes. One notable event that year saw the final working of a GN 2-4-0, No 4070, into London on 19 April with horseboxes. This veteran returned north next day with empty stock.

Use of GC 'B3' 4-6-0s on the Pullman trains between London and Leeds/Harrogate had not proved outstandingly successful. Because of their unsuitable firebox design giving rise to excessive coal consumption and steaming troubles, the class had been relegated to secondary main line duties on their native section. On the Pullman duties over GN lines, loads were not unduly heavy nor timings tight but the advent of the long 198.8 mile non-stop run of the 'Harrogate Pullman' between Harrogate and Kings Cross undoubtedly highlighted deficiencies. Officials directly concerned with operating these locomotives eventually persuaded W. G. P. Maclure to try a different GC class on the job. This turned out to be one of the 'Director' Class D11/2 built to LNER gauge in 1924 by Beyer Peacock for use in Scotland. No 6399 *Allan Bane* had been on trial over certain GE lines from late 1926 and in January 1927 it ran a successful trial with Leeds enginemen on the 'Harrogate Pullman', thus bringing another fresh class into Kings Cross. The upshot was not long delayed for on 14 February one of the original GC 'Improved Directors', No 5511 *Marne* moved from Gorton to Copley Hill, making its first trip with the Pullman two days later. Over the ensuing two months all six 'B3s' left the GN section for Gorton in exchange for two more 'D11s' Nos 5506/7 which went to Copley Hill and three Ivatt Atlantics,

Nos 3287 to Doncaster, plus Nos 4402/37 to Kings Cross. Thenceforth the 'B3' engines appeared at Kings Cross only on excursion trains mainly from the Grimsby or Lincoln districts but the 'Directors' did a good job on the Pullman duties for just over five years, during which time eight of the 10 engines in Class D11/1 were based at Copley Hill at various times.

Rivalry between East and West Coast Routes had been subdued for more than 30 years after the Race to Aberdeen in 1895. Formation of the two large Groups in 1923 when the two routes came under control of the London, Midland & Scottish (West Coast) and LNER (East Coast), caused an upturn in competition. This was first evident in 1927 when the LMS commenced running the 'Royal Scot' non-stop over the 236¼ miles from Euston to Carnforth. This spurred the LNER to book the relief 'Flying Scotsman' which operated at 9.50am from Kings Cross on Mondays, Thursdays, Fridays and Saturdays, non-stop between London and Newcastle, 268¼ miles. This new idea brought into being the first Newcastle Lodge Link at Kings Cross Top Shed, and the first regular workng to London by Gateshead engines and men. Preliminary trials took place on 10 May when 'A1' Pacific No 4474 *Victor Wild* went through from London to Newcastle on the 9.50am but made the customary booked stops. Next day Gateshead sent their crack 'A1' No 2569 *Gladiateur* through to London on the 'Flying Scotsman', possibly the first visit of a NE area Gresley Pacific to London, heralding a spate of regular workings by Tyneside Pacifics in future years. The first non-stop journey was made on 11 July 1927, when No 4475 *Flying Fox* driven by A. Pibworth took the 9.50 from Kings Cross to Newcastle in 5hr 30min and No 2569 *Gladiateur* with driver T. Blades of Gateshead made the second trip on Thursday 14 July. This non-stop run was made only in the northbound direction by Kings Cross engines and men on Mondays and Fridays and Gateshead on Thursdays and Saturdays. The balancing turn was 9.30 ex-Newcastle covered by the London engine on Tuesdays and Saturdays and Gateshead on Wednesdays and Fridays. This train made stops intermediately. During the few weeks of Summer service when this non-stop operated only five engines appeared; Nos 2552, 4474/5 of Kings Cross and Nos 2569/75 of Gateshead.

Four excursions from Scotland in connection with the International Football match England v Scotland, at Wembley on 31 March 1928 were all double headed into Kings Cross; Nos 736 ('C7'), and 2030 ('D20'); 2209 ('C7') and 1207 ('D20'); 2196 ('C7') and 2104 ('D20'); with 1794 ('C6') and 2198 ('C7') thus providing an interesting morning for the local observers.

Introduction of the Newcastle non-stop by the LNER in 1927 prompted the LMS to extend their run to 299 miles between Euston and Carlisle, using their newly built 'Royal Scot' 4-6-0s. This spurred the LNER to greater effort and plans were made to run the two 'Flying Scotsman' trains non-stop over the 392.7 miles between London and Edinburgh each way on weekdays during the 1928 summer service. Much preparatory work had to be undertaken in advance, most of which was in the NE Area. The problem of engine crews being available for such a long journey had been ingenuously overcome by Gresley, by designing a corridor tender to enable crew changes en route. Care had to be taken in the selection of engines for which a primary requirement was for those converted to long-travel valve gear. At the time only 21 Pacifics had this refinement and only one was at Kings Cross shed. So it was necessary for a number of transfers to be arranged. There could be no doubt as to which 'A1' Pacific should take the first Edinburgh non-stop from Kings Cross — No 4472 *Flying Scotsman*. Accordingly this engine was given long-travel valves and a corridor tender in April 1928 and transferred from Doncaster to Kings Cross in exchange for No 2553. Two Grantham 'A1s' Nos 2547 and 4476 also moved to Kings Cross, some confusion arose when No 2556 *Ormonde* emerged from Doncaster Plant with a corridor tender despite having short travel valves. It was sent to Kings Cross in exchange for No 2546 transferred to Grantham. The corridor tender was put on to No 2552 *Sansovino*, which had received the new valve gear and Nos 2546/56 returned to their original sheds.

Tuesday 1 May 1928, marking the inauguration of the world's record non-stop run of 392.7 miles between London and Edinburgh, was an unforgettable occasion for all GN enthusiasts. Large crowds assembled at Kings Cross to witness the first departure of the 10.00 'Flying Scotsman' train made up of a brand new train of 12 bogies, headed by an immaculate No 4472 *Flying Scotsman* in charge of driver A. Pibworth and fireman Goddard.

14
Down express on Langley troughs in 1925 behind 'A1' 4-6-2 No 4474 *Victor Wild*.
F. R. Hebron/Rail Archive Stephenson

15
'P1' 2-8-2 No 2394 at Langley with an up goods.
H. Gordon Tidey

16
Greenwood, 1923. Ex-GCR 'B3' 4-6-0 No 1165 *Valour* with the 17.35 down express. Still with GCR livery and number. *H. Gordon Tidey*

17
'P1' 2-8-2 No 2393 fitted with booster.
Ian Allan Library

18
Near Cemetery signalbox, 1924.
'D1' 4-4-0 No 60N piloting 'C1' 4-4-2 No 1441N on a down express.
Real Photos Co

19
An interesting train. The 'Welwyn Garden City Express' climbs to Potters Bar in September 1926 behind 'N7' 0-6-2T No 471. *H. Gordon Tidey*

20
Ivatt 'R1' 0-8-2T No 3117 at Kings Cross in 1926. *C. C. B. Herbert*

The relief crew travelling in the train until changing over at Tollerton, the half-way point beyond York, was driver T. Blades and fireman Morris of Gateshead. For many, like the author who was still at school there was no chance of seeing this great event, but most were out on the lineside just before 18.00 anxiously awaiting the passage of the up train, due into London at 18.15. The up main signals were pulled off but it seemed an eternity before the non-stop emerged from Barnet tunnel 2min early bringing into view a completely strange Pacific, No 2580 *Shotover* carrying a headboard on the smokebox with the train's name. This was something novel indeed for which Haymarket shed deserved congratulations. It was not long before the idea was copied by Kings Cross. The up run had been completed by driver Henderson and fireman McKenzie of Haymarket, relieved by driver Day and fireman Gray of Kings Cross. The excitement over, it was back indoors for us boys to try and concentrate on homework!

Next evening we saw No 4472 return but on Friday came a big surprise because the engine carried no number of its cab. Identified by the name it was *Donovan* (No 2546) hastily given a corridor tender so it could replace No 4472 whilst that engine had a suspect tender axle box repaired. Throughout the ensuing weeks the non-stop running was watched with care. We were not disappointed for in due course came more fresh Pacifics from Scotland; Nos 2573 *Harvester*, 2563 *William Whitelaw* and 2564 *Knight of the Thistle*. Top Shed Kings Cross used Nos 2552 *Sansovino*, 4475 *Flying Fox* and 4476 *Royal Lancer* as well as 4472.

On reflection it now seems certain that these events crystallised my enthusiasm for steam locomotives with an unashamed preference for Gresley Pacifics and Ivatt Atlantics, plus a desire to know the why and wherefore of railway working methods, train services and early history.

At the end of the 1928 summer service our attention was riveted on other events. The winter diagrams provided for the first time two daily lodging turns by Kings Cross and Gateshead engines and crews between London and Newcastle. The trains concerned were 'Flying Scotsman' each way plus 22.35 Kings Cross-Edinburgh Sleeping Car train and 23.00 Newcastle-Kings Cross. The No 1 link at Top Shed became known as the 'Newcastle Lodge Link' and consisted of six crews, each booked to a regular Pacific. On the day turn the 10.00 from London was taken to Newcastle (arrive 15.36). Whilst the men went into lodge their engine was prepared at Gateshead shed to work the 3.14 to Edinburgh in the hands of a Gateshead crew who worked it back to Newcastle on the up 'Flying Scotsman' at 10.00 from Edinburgh. On reaching Newcastle the London men took over their engine for the run on to Kings Cross. On the 22.35 night sleeping car train from London the engine went right through to Edinburgh with a crew change at Newcastle. Return south was on the 10.15 ex-Edinburgh as far as Newcastle where the engine was serviced at Gateshead shed in readiness for the 23.00 departure to London. Gateshead engines and men alternated on these duties. An unusual feature of the night turn was that the engines and men came off the up train at Grantham at 2.57 continuing to London (arrive 5.55) at 3.43. These particular diagrams were not popular with enginemen and lasted only until July 1931. It was not until another 23 years or so that night lodging diagrams appeared once more.

An unexpected visitor to Kings Cross shed for a seven month period between 29 September 1928 and 30 April 1929 was Class D49/1 4-4-0 No 245 *Lincolnshire*. During that time it was tried on a wide variety of GN Section passenger duties. One of its earliest runs was to Nottingham and back on 8 October with a race special. Subsequently it took turns on both 'Queen of Scots' and 'West Riding' Pullman diagrams to Leeds and return; on the 17.37 Hull express as far as Grantham, returning on a milk train; to Peterborough on the 7.45 'Parly' and return into Kings Cross at 13.05 on which train a slight mishap occurred one day when the driver's unfamiliarity with the Westinghouse/Vacuum ejector braking equipment caused him to hit the hydraulic buffer stops at Kings Cross. On 21 April 1930 No 245 working the up 'Queen of Scots' Pullman was timed over the 156.0 miles Doncaster-Kings Cross in 148 minutes and next day went down to Peterborough with the 16.15 semi-fast returning thence at 20.00 with the heavy 17.30 from Leeds express, normally a Pacific duty.

Visits by Class D49 engines thereafter were intermittent, mostly on excursions like on Cup Final day 1930 when both Nos 253/6 brought in 14-coach trains.

Normally Cambridge trains did not produce out

of the ordinary power at that time, but on 12 November 1928 the Royal train from Wolferton arrived at Kings Cross behind Class D16/1 'Super Claud' No 8783 which had been specially burnished for Royal duties along with No 8787. In October 1930 both these engines were transferred from Stratford to Cambridge and thereafter made regular runs to Kings Cross on weekdays arriving at 15.20 going back at 18.55 except when required for Royal train duties. Cambridge shed acquired its first examples of Gresley 'B17' 4-6-0s in November 1930 and lost little time in sending No 2819 *Welbeck Abbey* over the GN to London on the 15.20 arrival on 27 November. Rather more interest was aroused on Wednesday 15 October 1930 when Pacifics first worked through to Newmarket on race specials from Kings Cross. The 10.45 11-car Pullman was headed by Top Shed's favourite No 4475 *Flying Fox* followed at 11.00 by No 2561 *Minoru* on a 14-coach ordinary train. Thereafter whenever loads were above the Atlantic limit, Pacifics continued to work Newmarket specials until 1939.

Until the London Underground Piccadilly line was extended northward from Finsbury Park to Cockfosters via Wood Green and Southgate in 1932, the vast majority of persons living in the northern suburbs had to use the GN suburban services to reach London. These services reached their peak in the years 1920-32. Much needed relief was afforded by the extension of Piccadilly line trains to Cockfosters, enabling some slight reductions to be made in peak hour GN trains as well as easing overcrowding.

The focal point was Finsbury Park through which all trains to and from London terminal points had to pass. In 1929 between 8.00 and 10.00 75 suburban trains were handled there and in the evening peak from 17.00 until 19.00 there were 65.

There was a great deal of interchanging at Finsbury Park both morning and evening. In the morning three trains were handled between 8.13 and 8.16; the 7.32 Welwyn Garden City-Kings Cross (8.13-8.14); 7.31 Hertford North-Moorgate (8.14-8.15); 7.59 Alexandra Palace-Broad Street (8.14-8.16). These trains used the up fast, up slow and up branch lines respectively. Similar patterns were repeated at intervals throughout the peak.

Evening operations were often more hectic because the down side had three island platforms and four running lines. An interesting time to witness the efficient manner in which all grades of staff handled the very heavy traffic was between 18.00 and 18.30. Usually the stationmaster supervised operations standing on Platforms 7/8 in front of the train indicators. The Station Inspector, one of the old school of railwaymen, always neatly dressed and sporting a rose in season would be at the head of the same platforms while platforms 6/7 were in charge of a leading porter and No 10 of a foreman. Other staff were at strategic points to close doors and in summer time to turn off the gas lighting of Hertford line trains not going beyond Cuffley. Stations served by each train were called out in clear loud tones.

Between 18.17 and 18.23 no less than six trains departed. The 17.59 Moorgate-Gordon Hill and 18.11 Kings Cross-High Barnet left at 18.17. The 18.21 Finsbury-Park-Enfield Chase left from platform 10 and one minute later the 18.05 Broad Street-New Barnet from Nos 6/7 simultaneously with the 18.15 Kings Cross-Cambridge/ Peterborough from No 5. Finally at 18.23 the 18.05 Moorgate-Alexandra Palace left from Nos 8/9. Sometimes during this brief spell the 18.00 No 2 Express Goods Kings Cross-Leeds passed on the goods line west of the platforms. Invariably the 18.15 ex-Kings Cross was 'K3' hauled and each night would race the LMS 'Jinty' 0-6-0T on the 18.05 from Broad Street. Generally the latter had the best of it as far as Hornsey, on its non-stop sprint to New Southgate, but from then on the larger 'K3' had taken hold of its heavier load to draw rapidly away.

It will be clear that there was plenty of interest for the lineside observers. Within the space of 6min one could see four 'N2s', two 'K3s' and an LMS 'Jinty' leaving Finsbury Park in the midst of much hustle capably handled in a manner which would cause present day suburban travellers to turn green in envy!

For many years Kings Cross 'Top' shed housed some 70 'N2s', Hornsey had half a dozen and Hatfield only two or three to cover their inner suburban diagrams including Moorgate turns. Between them the three sheds covered all local trains and empty stock duties in the district. 'Top Shed' had 45 'N2s' in the 'regular Met Link' — all double shifted by crews who kept to their own engines as far as possible, thus ensuring a very high standard of performance and reliability. The remaining 'N2s' were used in the 'Odd Met Link' in which there were a few local train turns together with Kings

Cross station pilot, empty stock, Edgware branch passenger and goods and branch goods to Alexandra Palace and High Barnet. In addition to local passenger diagrams Hornsey undertook ecs and some shunting in carriage sidings. For a period in the mid-1930s there were a number of diagrams at Kings Cross taking 'N2s' to Baldock in the hands of men from a main line link. Hatfield worked to Kings Cross, Moorgate, Hertford via Cuffley with 'N2s'. The three branches radiating from Hatfield were worked independently of the main suburban services. On duties not involving Moorgate trains Hatfield used 'N7s' and on the through Dunstable duties generally Ivatt 4-4-0s until displaced by 'J6' 0-6-0s in 1936.

The Hornsey 'N1' 0-6-2T stood in for 'N2s' when required and usually had one evening turn from Finsbury Park to High Barnet but their main use was on the South London Goods transfer trips travelling via York Road (Kings Cross), Farringdon and Snow Hill to Blackfriars and beyond. When the 'Coronation' streamlined train was introduced in 1937 one Hornsey 'N1' was specially cleaned to haul the empty stock into Kings Cross each Monday-Friday afternoon.

21
'C1' 4-4-2 No 4419 with booster in action climbs Holloway bank with the 11.20 Edinburgh Pullman from Kings Cross in 1927.
F. R. Hebron/Rail Archive Stephenson

22
A special for filming purposes 'A1' 4-6-2 No 4472 *Flying Scotsman* at Palmers Green in 1929. Filming was carried out on the Hertford-Stevenage loop.
F. R. Hebron/Rail Archive Stephenson

23
'A3' 4-6-2 No 2580 *Shotover* at Kings Cross after working the first up Edinburgh non-stop on 1 May 1928. *LPC/Ian Allan Library*

24
'A1' 4-6-2 No 2546 *Donovan* at Kings Cross on 4 May 1928 after working the up 'Flying Scotsman'. Note absence of number on the cabside.
LPC/Ian Allan Library

25
'D3' 4-4-0 No 4311 pilots 'C1' 4-4-2 No 4460 on the 17.30 Kings Cross-Newcastle north of Potters Bar.
F. R. Hebron/Rail Archive Stephenson

26
An up Pullman train passes Potters Bar behind 'C1' 4-4-2 No 3301 on 30 March 1929.
E. R. Wethersett/Ian Allan Library

27
'D49/1' 4-4-0 No 245 *Lincolnshire* on Kings Cross shed in 1929. *LPC/Ian Allan Library*

28
'C1' 4-4-2 No 3279, as rebuilt with four cylinders in 1915, on a Yorkshire Coast express at Greenwood in 1930. *Real Photos*

29
'A1' 4-6-2 No 2570 *Tranquil* at Kings Cross, having worked a Newcastle-Kings Cross excursion. *LPC/Ian Allan Library*

30
LNER 4-6-2-2 No 10000 leaving Grantham with the up 'Flying Scotsman' in 1930.
F. R. Hebron/Rail Archive Stephenson

31
Royston, 18 August 1930. 'C2' 4-4-2 No 3260 on a Cambridge-Kings Cross stopping train.
E. R. Wethersett/Ian Allan Library

32
'D2' 4-4-0 No 3042 enters Brookmans Park station with a down semi-fast.
H. Gordon Tidey

1931-1939

Daily newspapers in December 1929 carried reports of a new, revolutionary steam locomotive, designed by Gresley and built at Darlington under conditions of great secrecy. The most remarkable feature of this engine, numbered 10000, was a water tube boiler enclosed in an air smoothed casing painted grey. It was immediately dubbed the 'Hush-Hush' engine. After some trial running in the North Eastern Area it was worked light to London on 7 January 1930 for official inspection. On my way to work next morning I was fortunate enough to see this monster on the Kings Cross station turntable about 8.00 being turned in readiness for a demonstration run to Hitchin and back. Two days later it left Kings Cross shed shortly after 7.30 running light back to Darlington. It next appeared in London on 13 February hauling a 500ton test train plus dynamometer car. Reaching Kings Cross at 15.12 it returned north next morning at 9.50 but was seen by very few observers.

After more trials in the north-east and Scotland the unique 4-6-4 was handed over to Gateshead shed on 20 June 1930. On 31 July GN observers were surprised to see it arrive on time at Kings Cross with the non-stop 'Flying Scotsman', loaded to 11 bogies and driven by J. G. Eltringham one of Gateshead's best enginemen. Special arrangements had to be made on this run for Gateshead men to handle the engine throughout from Edinburgh to London so another crew worked between Edinburgh and Tollerton. After returning north next day with the 10.00 non-stop it was nearly a year before we saw No 10000 again.

On 30 April 1931 the 'Flying Scotsman' reached Kings Cross nearly 30min late behind No 10000 which had been sent south to take part in a Railway Exhibition at Norwich on 2/3 May. The engine ran light from Top Shed on 1 May to Bounds Green,

thence via Palace Gates and South Tottenham to Stratford followed later by 'A1' No 4472 *Flying Scotsman*. Regrettably the onward progress of these two engines from Stratford to Norwich does not seem to have been recorded. Both returned to Kings Cross by the same route on 5 May and next day went north en route to another exhibition at Nottingham. Many such exhibitions were staged by the LNER in the next few years presenting a varied selection of locomotives and rolling stock to the public in which No 10000 was often included.

So far as the GN Section was concerned Gresley's experimental 4-6-4 made its final appearance in the week commencing 20 May 1931 when it completed three round trips between Newcastle and London on the 'Junior Scotsman' which ran up 15min behind the non-stop main train to reach Kings Cross at 18.15 and went north at 10.05. By all accounts the Gateshead enginemen had some anxious moments during that week when timekeeping was not exemplary. From then on the 'W1' in its original form remained on purely internal NE Area duties interspersed with long periods of inactivity at Darlington Works.

33
Kings Cross shed yard on 18 April 1931. To the fore is 'C1' 4-4-2 No 3288, left is 'K3' 2-6-0 No 135.
E. R. Wethersett/Ian Allan Library

Certain days in the first half of each year never failed to bring GN line observers to the lineside very early on Saturday mornings or perhaps around midnight. These were the occasions of International football matches when England played Scotland and the FA and Rugby League Cup Finals all of which were staged at Wembley bringing many extra trains into Kings Cross, often with unusual locomotives.

A typical year was 1930 when all three events took place at Wembley. For the Rugby match on 15 March seven specials arrived between 7.00 and 12.12, bringing three Gateshead Pacifics ('A1' Nos 2574/7/95); three NE Atlantics (Nos 2196/7, 2205), and one 'D11' from Leeds (No 5506). Owing to heavy loads on the return journey No 2196 was assisted by GN 'C1' Atlantic No 3251 and No 2205 by 'C2' No 3255. The latter pair hauling 510ton. On 5 April the Association Football match attracted 16 specials, nine of them from Scottish stations and all Pacific hauled throughout from Edinburgh to Kings Cross. Most were heavy formations of 13-15 bogies and engines were from Haymarket (No 2564), Gateshead (Nos 2568/70/2/3/4/6) and Heaton (Nos 2579/82) — a veritable feast of Pacifics all on one day! Two Newcastle trains had Raven Atlantics ('C7' Nos 2196/2210); one from Leeds had their favourite 'Director' No 5506 *Butler Henderson*; from Grimsby came 'B3' No 6164 *Earl Beatty* hauling 14 coaches whilst Doncaster engines brought in specials from Hull ('A1' No 2555), West Riding ('A1' No 4481) and Gainsborough ('C1' No 3273).

As always the big event was FA Cup Final day when many die-hard enthusiasts rose somewhere around 4.00 to reach their nearest vantage point in time to see most, if not all, specials emanating from diverse places between Tyneside and Burton-on-Trent. 26 April 1930 provided 24 extra trains into Kings Cross scheduled between 3.49 (Hull) and 10.33 (Doncaster). Principal interest that day centred on two 'D49' 'Shire' 4-4-0s Nos 253 *Oxfordshire* and 256 *Hertfordshire* on trains from Middlesbrough (410ton) and Saltburn (400ton) respectively. Both had to take assistance on the return journey at night, No 253 by 'Klondyke' 'C2' No 3252 and No 256 by 'D2' 4-4-0 No 4391. Only three Gateshead Pacifics appeared (Nos 2570/3/7) and four NE Atlantics (Nos 2168/96, 2208/10). The seemingly inevitable No 5506 from Leeds and No 6164 from Grimsby also appeared. For many of us a highlight on Cup Final days were the through excursions from Burton-on-Trent, Derby and Pinxton bringing Colwick 'K2' 2-6-0s into London, not a normal thing otherwise. On this occasion the three trains were headed by Nos 4646, 4640 and 4643 respectively each well before time and nicely groomed. From Lincoln came a 'B7' 4-6-0 No 5480 and 'K3' 2-6-0 No 4000 whilst another 'K3' No 109 came from Gainsborough. The remainder being made up of Doncaster engines (Pacifics Nos 2544, 4470/3 and 'C1' No 4452) plus Peterborough 'C1s' Nos 4417/8. A typical Cup Final selection for the period, providing plenty of excitement for the faithful fans.

By comparison the Rugby League Final on 3 May was rather unexciting. Eleven specials were brought up by Doncaster Pacifics Nos 2544, 2743, 4471/7/80/1 and Atlantics Nos 4452/3. For a change Leeds sent 'D11' No 5511 *Marne* and Sheffield shed provided 'B2' 4-6-0 No 5423 *Sir Sam Fay* for a train from Farnworth. Unusually for such an occasion Grantham Pacific No 4478 brought in a special.

After the notable events in the first nine years of LNER operations together with the onset of severe economic depression the next few years were comparably calm. Fewer unusual locomotives were seen. Of the first production batch of new 'A3' Super Pacifics, Kings Cross had received three, Nos 2744 *Grand Parade*, 2746 *Fairway* and 2750 *Papyrus*. None went to Grantham shed which relied entirely on 'A1s' for their share of the heaviest East Coast trains but Doncaster had Nos 2743 *Felstead*, 2747 *Coronach*, 2751 *Humorist* and 2752 *Spion Kop*.

In July 1931 driver W. Sparshatt who had been in Pullman links at Kings Cross Top Shed since 1924, was promoted to No 1 Link (Newcastle Lodge) replacing B. Glasgow who retired. The six drivers in No 1 Link with regular engines were: D. Miles (4472), F. Perry (2746), T. Toplis (2547), W. Holland (4475), H. Gutteridge (2750) and W. Sparshatt (4476). Their roster included the two lodge turns to Newcastle leaving Kings Cross at 10.00 and 10.05 (the former was actually to Edinburgh on the non-stop Flying Scotsman which they drove as far as Tollerton); 7.45 and 10.20 stopping trains to Peterborough with return arrivals in London at 13.05 and 16.30 on expresses; 15.00 to Grantham returning with the 22.05 'Mid-day

34
'B12' 4-6-0 No 8527 on an up Cambridge express at Potters Bar on 18 August 1931.
E. R. Wethersett/Ian Allan Library

35
A rare instance on the GN main line of a Pacific being piloted — 'C1' 4-4-2 No 4446 and an 'A3' No 2596 *Manna* at New Southgate with the 11.30 Kings Cross-Edinburgh. *E. Neve collection*

36
'A3' 4-6-2 No 2751 *Humorist* (with experimental smoke deflection) on a Yorkshire-Kings Cross express in 1933.
H. Gordon Tidey

Scotsman' and finally 22.50 parcels/mails to Peterborough returning on a similar train due into Kings Cross at 4.52. Kings Cross No 1A 'Leeds Pullman' link contained six drivers also each with a booked 'C1' Atlantic. Their duties were 10.00 Sunday Pullman to Leeds — 16.45 Tu/Th; 11.15 'Queen of Scots' MWF and 16.45 MWF all lodging at Leeds. Their short turns were 4.45 Leeds Mail to Peterborough arriving back at 10.24 semi-fast; 17.00 semi-fast to Grantham — Meat train due East Goods 23.12 and 17.10 Baldock and 22.45 return. Nine drivers comprised the No 2 Express Passenger Link, popularly known as the Pacific and Atlantic. These men used the spare Pacifics on turns to Grantham or Peterborough, including the 19.30 'Aberdonian' and Atlantics on the 7.10 to Cambridge; 5.02 to Peterborough and 8.45 to Grantham. They also manned the three Main Line Pilot turns in Kings Cross station each 24 hours on weekdays, maintaining an Atlantic in steam on the stand in the locomotive yard in case of emergency.

Amongst unusual engine workings at this time was the use by Doncaster of 'B17' 'Sandringhams' on excursions from Lincoln. Nos 2835 *Milton* and 2833 *Kimbolton Castle* were seen on 5 September and 31 October 1931 respectively.

Despite the increased number of Pacifics in service it was still possible to see double headed trains, especially at peak holiday times. Normally these were either 4-4-0 plus 4-4-2 or pairs of large Atlantics, both combinations being officially permitted. Much less common was a piloted Pacific, allowed only in emergency and subject to speed restriction across Welwyn Viaduct. The 20.25 Mail from Kings Cross loaded heavily at times causing strange combinations like 'C1' No 4418 plus 'K3' No 4008 and 'C1' No 4417 plus 'K3' No 163 on separate occasions.

A less well known source of unusual combinations was the 8.05 stopping train to Hitchin on Saturdays which had two engines as far as Hatfield where the front one was detached in order to work a Baldock slow later. Some notable recordings were 'D3' 4-4-0 No 4301 plus 'K3' 2-6-0 No 4009; 'D3' No 4346 plus 'A5' 4-6-2T No 5129; 'C2s' Nos 3255 plus 3982; 'D16/2' No 8783 plus 'C1' No 3279; 'N2' 0-6-2T No 2666 plus 'C2' No 3250. On other days the 8.05 was used to run-in engines after repair as in July/August 1933 when NE Atlantics Nos 716, 2195 and 2204 were all seen.

After the trials in 1923 by No 2400, Raven Pacifics were not often seen at Kings Cross. They did sometimes come up on the 'Flying Scotsman' when the booked London engine was not available at Newcastle as on 5 April 1930 when No 2401 appeared. A more remarkable occasion was on 5 May 1931 when No 2402 arrived with the 5.55 from Newcastle but failed to return at 22.35 as booked. Next day it took the 20.25 Mail to Peterborough with a Kings Cross crew, returned on the 3.45 Mail and then went home to Newcastle at 22.35 on 7 May.

Over the years 1923-31 very little change had taken place in express train schedules but signs of impending change came in December 1931 when a trial run was arranged using the 14.48 Peterborough-Kings Cross (through coaches from Cromer M&GN). 'C1' No 3295 was selected with driver W. Sparshatt who ran the 76.4 miles start to stop in 71min 10sec inclusive of a 10mile/h slack at New Southgate. The maximum speed was 84mile/h at Offord. This was followed on 10 December by a similar test using 'A1' Pacific No 2547 *Doncaster* when Sparshatt completed the journey in 66min 10sec also with the 10mile/h slack. A maximum of 92mile/h was attained at New Barnet. In each case the load was 285tons (seven coaches).

Next, on 16 December, Doncaster shed was afforded the opportunity to show what could be done by a Super Pacific. The engine was No 2743 *Felstead* driven by Watson on the 7.50 ex-Leeds 'Breakfast Flyer' loaded to 310tons. On this train the 105.5 miles Grantham-Kings Cross were run in the unprecedented time of 92min 42sec. These fast runs heralded sweeping reductions in all express schedules over the East Coast main line from 2 May 1932, including 25min off the winter 'Flying Scotsman' to Edinburgh and 45min from the summer non-stop working. Pullmans also shared in the cuts, having 156min schedules each way over the 156.0 miles between London and Doncaster. Undoubtedly the most notable reduction was 15min off the 7.50 from Leeds which, with stops at Retford and Grantham, was allowed 160min from Doncaster to London. The culmination of this train's weekday run was a 100min sprint over the 105.5 miles from Grantham — 63.3mile/h average which was then the highest average speed in Europe for any non-stop run over 100 miles.

Precious little chance of fast running came the way of Grantham shed until this time when the 8.30 'Mark Lane Express' from there to Kings Cross, which they worked MX, was allowed but 78min for the 76.4 miles Peterborough-London including a stop at Huntingdon whence the 58.9 miles had to be run in 57min.

Departure times of main line trains were little altered but most arrivals were 10-15min earlier causing lineside observers to adjust their habits. The effect on punctuality gave rise to speculation, in the event timekeeping was usually good. Enginemen throughout the main line shared in these accelerations so there was plenty of competition between sheds concerned and indeed between drivers themselves.

Time honoured engine diagrams were largely unaltered except for the through Newcastle turns on which Heaton shed took a share for the first time, alternating with Kings Cross working the 10.00 'Flying Scotsman' and 8.00 from Newcastle to London. This diagram brought regular visits, up M/W/F and down Tu/Th/S by the five Heaton Pacifics Nos 2578 *Bayardo*, 2579 *Dick Turpin*, 2580 *Shotover*, 2581 *Neil Gow* and 2582 *Sir Hugo* hitherto rarely seen in the south. The night train lodging turn had been abandoned in July 1931 so from May 1932 Gateshead shared with Kings Cross the 13.20 and 17.30 down with inward arrivals at 17.50 ('Flying Scotsman') and 21.55.

One significant change in locomotive working did occur on the 'Queen of Scots' Pullman which had a 195min non-stop booking from Leeds-Kings Cross. This proved rather too much for the 'D11' 'Director' 4-4-0s which had coped successfully since 1927. Therefore this class was replaced at Copley Hill shed by three large Atlantics which were still capable of maintaining, or even cutting, this exacting time. Only three sets of men comprised the Copley Hill Pullman link then each booked to their own engine — Nos 3280 (driver Bird), 4423 (Rogers) and 4433 (Malthouse). From then on the Top Shed Pullman crews had to look to their laurels in the light of stiff competition from the Yorkshire men who are on record in achieving many excellent runs.

Apart from the glamour of the East Coast expresses there was a welcome revision of Cambridge express services. These had seen very little improvement since the turn of the century but in 1932 five new expresses were put on each way on weekdays, carrying roofboards inscribed 'Garden Cities and Cambridge Buffet Express'. Each set train comprised three vehicles in which the third class had armrests dividing the seats into three — a novelty then — and one coach was open with a buffet and seating for partaking meals. Stops were made in either direction at Welwyn Garden City, Hitchin and Letchworth. The standard schedule was 82min down and 77min up, reduced in 1933 to 75 and 72min respectively whilst two trains made an extra stop at Royston for which only 2min were allowed. Such was the popularity of these two trains — soon dubbed 'Beer Trains' by Cambridge Undergraduates and other regular users. Five trains each way ran on weekdays. At first departures from Kings Cross were at 9.30, 12.40 (12.10SO), 14.00, 19.45 and 23.40. From Cambridge times were: 9.20, 12.25, 15.25, 17.20 and 22.05. The three coach formations quickly grew to six or more. Curiously no special provision had been made for locomotives to work these extra trains so a wide variety appeared in the first few weeks. Large Ivatt and small Atlantics and 4-4-0s; GE 'Clauds' and 'B12' 4-6-0s were all pressed into service. Soon some additional Atlantics were transferred to Cambridge where an enlarged link was formed of eight crews sharing four 'C1s' between them. Cambridge was responsible for seven of the 10 'Buffet Express' workings whilst Kings Cross No 2 link had the 9.20 down and 12.25 up also the 22.05 up. Many fine runs were made by drivers from both sheds on these services on which the Ivatt Atlantics found a new lease of life. A favourite Saturday jaunt for some North London enthusiasts was to take the 16.15 ex-Kings Cross down to Hatfield, usually behind a Top Shed Pacific. Changing there into a local service to Welwyn Garden City to return on the 18.13 'Buffet Express' for a 24min non-stop sprint to London. Many unforgettable trips were had with Cambridge drivers running their Atlantics with skill and verve.

Something unusual in East Coast rail travel came on Friday 16 June 1933 when at 23.20 the first 'Northern Belle' train 'Cruise' left Kings Cross. The seven day itinerary took in some of Scotland's most scenic routes by rail and included daytime coach tours as well as a Clyde Coast steamer trip to the Kyles of Bute. The inclusive cost of this venture was £20, covering all meals and first class accommodation on the train; probably the best bargain ever offered by a British railway.

37
A retouched photograph of 'P2' 2-8-2 No 2001 *Cock o' The North* on a Leeds-Kings Cross express near Welwyn Garden City.

38
'O2' 2-8-0 No 3481 on an up goods near Potters Bar.
Ian Allan Library

39
'K3' 2-6-0 No 153 on the 15.40 down Scotch goods passes Cemetery box on 11 June 1932.
E. R. Wethersett/Ian Allan Library

40
Mailbags at the lineside near Hatfield wait to be collected by a down express and mail train headed by 'K3' 2-6-0 No 4009, still fitted with GN-style cab.

41
'A4' 4-6-2 No 2509 *Silver Link*, in original livery with painted name, on the 16.15 down Grantham semi-fast at New Southgate in September 1935. *E. Neve*

42
A cross-London goods at Wandsworth Road, SR behind 'N1' 0-6-2T No 1587. *H. Gordon Tidey*

The 15-coach formation included: brake first plus sleeping car for train staff; open first; two first dining cars; kitchen car; cocktail bar and hairdressing saloon coach from the 'Flying Scotsman' set; six sleeper firsts and two full brakes containing luggage lockers. Total tare weight being 550ton. Over the initial stages of the route to Edinburgh, Pacific haulage was possible but on other lines double heading was necessary except where it was possible to detach the sleeping cars and brakes during daytime journeys. Three trips ran in 1933 during June.

For the 1934 season one of the full brakes was dispensed with reducing the weight to 507ton. The itinerary was slightly amended to commence at Harrogate on the first day, instead of Edinburgh, and on the final day the train ran direct from Newcastle to York instead of via the coast to Northallerton. Departure on Fridays was advanced to 21.20 and on the initial 1934 run the engine from Kings Cross to Beverley was 'A1' Pacific No 2546 *Donovan*.

Operation of this train continued until 1939, usually for four weeks in June. Its popularity was unquestioned.

In May 1934 the first Gresley Mikado passenger engine, Class P2 No 2001 *Cock o' the North* emerged from Doncaster Plant. On 31 May it ran light up to London for official inspection next day. It was then sent over to the GE Section at Ilford for inclusion in an exhibition on 2 June, where it stayed only one day. At 9.20 on Sunday 3 June the giant engine was seen on the connecting line between Palace Gates and Bounds Green GN sidings where it reversed and ran tender first through Wood Green before crossing to the down main line to set off northwards.

The new 'P2' next appeared at Kings Cross taking the 10.20 stopping train to Peterborough, returning into London with the Edinburgh express at 16.15 on 12/14/16 June. Then, on 19 June, a test train of 650ton including Dynamometer car was taken from Kings Cross to Barkston and back. In the course of this trial the haulage potential of this fine locomotive was ably demonstrated by Top Shed driver C. Peachey. Next day No 2001 was back on the 10.20 with driver Sparshatt and on the following day returned to Doncaster on the 13.30 West Riding express. Further dynamometer tests took place between 2 and 11 July using service trains, usually the 11.04 ex-Doncaster and 16.00 from Kings Cross return — all with Doncaster drivers.

No 2001 was fitted with Poppet valve gears but the second 'P2', No 2002 *Earl Marischal*, received conventional piston valves and Walschaerts gear. It was first recorded on the 17.45 from Kings Cross on 27 October 1934, remaining at Doncaster until late May 1935, frequently working the 16.00 or 17.45 out of Kings Cross. It was joined by No 2001 from 15 April after that engine had returned from trials in France. There were occasions when both were at Kings Cross on the same day, one on the 16.00 and the other leaving at 17.45.

An unusual feature on 14 April 1934 was the through working of three Scottish Pacifics on Football excursions. 'A1s' Nos 2566 *Ladas* and 2567 *Sir Visto* of Dundee shed and to the delight of all observers 'A3' No 2745 *Captain Cuttle* of Carlisle on a special ex-Aberdeen. Although No 2566 had worked to London on the non-stop 'Flying Scotsman' in 1928 and No 2745 had travelled to London on Doncaster duties in the same year, neither had been seen by many Londoners and no record exists of a previous visit by No 2567. Apart from the customary galaxy of Tyneside Pacifics other notable visitors that day were rebuilt Raven Atlantic No 732, then classed C7/2, and 'D49/2' *The Bedale*.

During 1934 the LNER began to evaluate the possibilities of high speed trains similar to those in operation on German railways where a diesel engined unit named the 'Flying Hamburger' had met with success. Gresley maintained that the same results could be achieved by steam locomotives and to prove his point test runs were organised. The first on 30 November 1934 was to Leeds and back using 'A1' No 4472 *Flying Scotsman*, capably handled by driver W. Sparshatt and fireman Webster who had by then acquired the famous engine as their regular mount. A light train of Dynamometer car plus three ordinary coaches weighing 145ton was required to complete the 185.8-mile non-stop run in 165min. Suffice to say that after topping Potters Bar summit at 67mph and passing Hitchin (31.9 miles) in 28min 22sec, the GN racing ground down to Huntingdon produced a maximum of 95mile/h. Peterborough (76.4mile) was passed in the unprecedented time of 60min 39sec and Stoke summit breasted at 81mile/h. Leeds was reached in 151min 56sec thus making a record destined to stand for another

30 years — well into the diesel era. For the return journey two more coaches were added, making the load up to 207ton. After passing Grantham (80.3 miles) in 70min 18sec, Sparshatt opened out his famous engine to advantage. Passing Stoke at 68½mile/h speed steadily increased until a maximum speed of 100mile/h was recorded between Little Bytham and Essendine, thus achieving the first *authenticated* 100mile/h by steam traction. The final stages of this run were taken more easily in view of Fireman Webster's notable effort causing him to tire. Kings Cross was reached in 157min 17sec. So ended an outstanding feat by the 180lb pressure Pacific which must have given great satisfaction to Gresley and his team. No less than to the enthusiast fraternity of the GN line who were now able to justify their faith in Gresley's Pacifics against any claims made by supporters of other locomotives.

Following the trial run to Leeds in November 1934 a decision was taken to institute a high speed steam hauled train on the Newcastle-London section commencing in September 1935. To obtain information in this connection a test was made from Kings Cross to Newcastle and back on 5 March 1935. This time the selected engine was a 220lb pressure 'A3' No 2750 *Papyrus* handled by Driver H. Gutteridge and fireman Wightman to whom the engine was regularly booked in the Kings Cross No 1 link. The load was six coaches weighing 217ton inclusive of the Dynamometer car. The planned schedule was observed closely without exceeding 88½mile/h (at Three Counties) to pass Peterborough in 63min 21sec and maintain 77½mile/h at Stoke summit. A severe setback occurred at Doncaster where speed had to be reduced to walking pace to pick up a pilotman who accompanied the train past the scene of a derailed goods train near Arksey which made single line working essential. Just north of Doncaster there was a dead stand for 19sec but from Arksey onwards a fine piece of acceleration on dead level track took them through York (188.2miles) only one minute late in 165min 11sec. Across the Great Plain of York speeds ranged between 79-85mile/h. After two severe slowings beyond Durham Newcastle was reached in 237min 7sec just under 3min early. The net time for the 268.3miles was 230min.

Examination of *Papyrus* revealed every bearing to be quite cool so the engine was prepared for the return journey to London in charge of driver Sparshatt and fireman Webster. After a rather slow start the 55.4 miles from Ferryhill to Poppleton Jct were covered in 41min 28sec with speed ranging from 80-88mile/h for 33 miles. Passing Shaftholme Jct 4min early speed was reduced past the scene of the earlier derailment, thus making the train right time past Doncaster. No unusual speeds were attempted onwards to Grantham but the schedule was closely maintained. Then, as on the previous test, Sparshatt opened out No 2750, topping Stoke summit at 69mile/h, and accelerating rapidly until a maximum of 108mile/h was reached. A new record of 62min 6sec was set for the 76.4 miles Peterborough-Kings Cross in the course of which the 27.0 miles Huntingdon-Hitchin, mainly uphill, occupied but 20min 17sec with a maximum of 87mile/h near Sandy. The overall time from Newcastle to Kings Cross was 231min 45sec a gain of 8min 15sec on schedule.

Because the date and approximate timing of this trial were known in advance a large number of enthusiasts gathered on No 1 platform at Kings Cross to witness the arrival shortly after 19.30. When it was announced that 108mile/h had been attained and Gresley had personally congratulated the enginemen, much applause arose. The select band of local observers knew that driver Sparshatt would be travelling home to New Barnet on the 20.15 local train, so gathered with him in one compartment. Despite his obvious tiredness he gave us his autograph.

Four specially designed Pacifics were ordered in March 1935 for working the high speed Newcastle service. Strict secrecy surrounded their construction making advance information unobtainable. A few fortunate people witnessed the arrival of the first 'A4' Pacific No 2509 *Silver Link* running light to Top Shed on 13 September 1935. It became known that the new Pacific would take the 7.10 slow train to Cambridge next morning. So I was up early and at the lineside awaiting its passage on the slow line. On a sunny September morning the sleek lines of the fully streamlined engine compelled admiration, but left a sense of dismay at the absence of traditional outlines. After progressing to the customary running-in turns to Peterborough at 7.45 and 16.15, arriving back in London at 13.05 and 21.15, No 2509 returned to Doncaster for a trial run with the complete train set on 20 September. In honour of the 25 years reign of King George

43
New Southgate. A down stopping train is headed by 'N2' 0-6-2T No 4747, with GNR articulated suburban stock.
Ian Allan Library

44
The new 'V2' 2-6-2 No 4771 *Green Arrow* climbs through New Southgate in 1936 with the Scotsman' goods. *E. Neve*

45
Ex-North Eastern Railway 4-4-2 No 2204 enters Kings Cross station on an up Cup Final special in 1936.
C. R. L. Coles

46
'B17' 4-6-0 No 2847 *Helmingham Hall* brings the empty stock of a GE Section train into Peterborough North station in 1936. *E. Neve*

47
'V2' 2-6-2 No 4774 passes New Southgate in 1937 with the 16.05 down Cleethorpes. *E. Neve*

48
Sir Nigel Gresley alongside 'A4' 4-6-2 No 4498.

49
Brookmans Park, 7 August 1937. The 16.05 down Cleethorpes express behind 'V2' 2-6-2 No 4774. *E. R. Wethersett/Ian Allan Library*

V and Queen Mary the train was named the 'Silver Jubilee' and the four streamlined locomotives carried names with a silver theme.

Friday 27 September 1935 was selected for a demonstration run by the complete train, conveying LNER officials, invited guests and the Press. Leaving Kings Cross at 14.25 it soon became apparent to the privileged occupants that something unusual was about to happen. Speed at Wood Green was 70mile/h increasing to 75 at Potters Bar. A totally unprecedented speed of 95mile/h through Hatfield gave passengers a nasty shock when the specially designed suspension system imparted sharp jerks due to excessive flexibility of side control springs. At mile post 30 between Stevenage and Hitchin speed crossed the magic 100. Then for no less than 25 miles down the famous racing stretch, where Stirling Singles had attained 80mile/h half a century before and Ivatt Atlantics produced 88/90mile/h with light loads, this amazing engine ran at 100mile/h or over. At Arlesey the peak speed of 112½mile/h was attained but not until the approach to severe curves beside the river Great Ouse near Offord did any slackening occur. The driver, A. J. Taylor, of Kings Cross later told how Gresley went on the footplate and said 'Steady on old chap, do you know you have touched 112 miles an hour?'. From then on the train proceeded normally to Barkston where it was turned on the triangle and returned to London. Needless to say large numbers of observers were at Kings Cross to witness its arrival. No Gresley supporter will ever forget the sight of the Chief Mechanical Engineer as he descended from the footplate, waving his 'Chronograph of vast dimensions' as it was described, and excitedly exclaiming '112 miles an hour!'. Deservedly it must have been a most satisfactory day for him.

Increasing patronage of the Bergen Line Shipping Co's Newcastle-Oslo sailing made necessary to provide extra trains on summer Fridays/Saturdays between Newcastle Tyne Commission Quay and Kings Cross. From 1933 the southbound train reached Kings Cross at 16.10 Fridays, usually in charge of a York NE Atlantic with York men. After lodging overnight these returned northwards at 13.05 on Saturdays. During June/July 1933 Nos 716, 2195/9 were recorded. Because the 13.05 load was often over 400ton an assisting engine was sometimes provided. Examples on record are 'C1' No 4432 plus 'C7' 2195; 'C2' 3255 plus 'C7' 2199. In 1935 this York duty persisted but was sometimes given a different northbound working as on 22 June when 'C7' No 2195 took the 11.30 semi-fast from Kings Cross to York and on the following Saturday Raven Pacific No 2402 went north with the 9.20 Scotch express, as did No 2404 on 6 July. This latter engine also came to London at 6.03 on Saturday 22 June and returned at 22.53 the same night with a Newcastle express. Thus the Raven Pacifics began to make more frequent appearances in London following transfer of the whole class to York. In 1936 the 13.05 duty SO had become a Gateshead 'A1' turn.

Introduction of the 'Silver Jubilee' streamlined express resulted in changes to the 'Harrogate Pullman' service which became the 'Yorkshire Pullman' serving Harrogate, Halifax and Hull. The normal 8-car formation was too heavy for Ivatt Atlantics to run non-stop over 156 miles Doncaster-Kings Cross at an overall 60mile/h average so the new train became a Doncaster duty each way over that section. The famed Kings Cross No 1A Leeds Pullman Link was disbanded and the six crews were absorbed into No 2 Link. Doncaster No 1 Link was increased to 10 crews and the new Pullman turn reaching London at 15.00 and returning at 16.45 became their crack job. The 'Queen of Scots' and 'Harrogate Sunday Pullman' trains were covered by Copley Hill shed still using Atlantics. The Pullman link at Leeds was increased to four crews booked to regular engines; Nos 3280 (driver Bird), 4423 (Rogers), 4433 (Malthouse) and 4460 (Berridge). The latter engine having been transferred from Kings Cross.

A very unusual locomotive working occurred on Saturday 18 April 1936 when the 'Flying Scotsman' reached Kings Cross behind 'C1' No 4448 piloting 'A3' No 2595 *Trigo*. More remarkably this pair returned north on the 11.30 Scotch expresses next morning. Normally double heading of Pacifics was prohibited across Welwyn viaduct, except in emergency subject to restricted speeds. Although there had been occasions when Pacifics working up express had been assisted into London due to shortage of steam, it was virtually unknown for a Pacific hauled down train to be piloted. Fortunately a photograph of this notable event has survived but not the explanation.

Britain's first streamlined train, the 'Silver Jubilee' went into service on Monday 30 September 1935. Leaving Newcastle at 10.00 on Mondays to Fridays it called at Darlington from 10.40-10.42. Thence the 232.3 miles to Kings Cross were booked in 198min at an average speed of 70.4mile/h. After arrival in London at 14.00 the stock was taken out to Holloway for servicing in readiness for the return trip commencing at 17.30. Darlington was reached at 20.48 and Newcastle at 21.30. Kings Cross Top shed was responsible for all locomotive working. To cover the additional duties two extra sets of men were added to No 1 Newcastle Lodge Link making a total of eight sets in the link. On Sundays the engine went north with the 12.40 express to Newcastle in readiness for Monday's 10.00 from there and on Saturdays the engine off Friday's down 'Silver Jubilee' worked home on the 'Flying Scotsman'. For the first two weeks only one 'A4' was available for high speed work, so No 2509 *Silver Link* carried out all the duties with conspicuous success. Bearing in mind that the enginemen had no previous experience of such high speed running it is worth recording that they did an excellent job right from the start.

Eventually three 'A4' Pacifics were allocated to Kings Cross, Nos 2509 *Silver Link*, 2510 *Quicksilver* and 2512 *Silver Fox*. The fourth engine No 2511 *Silver King* was sent to Gateshead shed to act as spare in case of need.

To share the locomotive duties worked on a lodging basis between London and Newcastle, Gateshead took over the daily working of the 13.20 afternoon Scotsman from London and worked the up 'Flying Scotsman' each day except Saturday.

Arrival of three 'A4' Pacifics at Top Shed enabled two large Atlantics, Nos 3286 and 4451 to be transferred to Hitchin for use on outer suburban work and indirectly resulted in the withdrawal of 'Klondyke' No 3982 from Hitchin in November 1935.

Between August and November 1935 the North British Locomotive Co built a batch of 'K3' 2-6-0s numbered in the 24xx series. The bulk of these 20 engines were put to work in the Southern Area of the LNER, five came to Kings Cross where they replaced older 'K3s' in No 3 Express Goods Link. So far as possible each driver in this link was booked to a regular engine. Their duties were mainly to Peterborough and back including the 'Three-Forty Scotsman' fast goods together with five similar trains; two fish empties and one parcels train. Six turns were at night and they also worked the 8.05 stopping train to Hitchin, but not usually with a 'K3'.

Early July 1936 brought the first Gresley 'V2' 2-6-2 *Green Arrow* to Kings Cross shed where its potential was quickly realised. On Saturdays in the peak summer season it often made two return trips to Peterborough, leaving Kings Cross with the 7.45 stopping train and getting back at 13.03 on a Leeds express and going down again on the 16.15 semi-fast to return at 21.25 with the 17.30 ex-Leeds express. On 25 July No 4771 made two return runs to Grantham taking the 12.05 Leeds relief and getting back at 17.43 conveying Aberdeen and Perth sections normally included on the 'Junior Scotsman'. At 22.53 *Green Arrow* set out once more to Grantham with the 565ton Newcastle portion of the 22.45 express and was back in London at 5.55 Sunday morning. Afterwards the new engine's regular weekday duty was to take the 15.40 'Scotsman' a fast braked goods to Peterborough whence it returned with the Hull fish due into East Goods at 21.22. GN line recorders had certainly had their fair share of new locomotive classes in the previous two years but the traditional clean-cut Gresley features of the first 'V2' made it an instant favourite. Three months later No 4774 was allocated to New England (Peterborough) where it went into service on the 15.40 fast goods from Kings Cross which it took over from No 4771, working through to York and returning to Peterborough on the 20.00 ex-Newcastle mail leaving York at 22.20. At weekends No 4774 often worked up to Kings Cross with special passenger trains and was seen on the 16.05 Cleethorpes express. On Sundays it came south with the 'Aberdonian' sleeping car express and returned at 12.00 on a Leeds express.

The long reign of Ivatt 4-4-0s at Hatfield shed began to decline during 1936 when 'D2' Nos 3041/2 were transferred away and replaced by two 'J6' superheated 0-6-0s, Nos 3590/1, for use on through Dunstable-London passenger trains, including the 17.54 with its tight 13min booking over the eight mile non-stop sprint from Finsbury Park to Hadley Wood, mostly uphill.

Production of further 'A4' Pacifics commenced late in 1936. The first of them, No 4482 *Golden Eagle* came to Kings Cross in December when it then carried lined green livery as did the next five of this series. In January 1937 two of the best Top Shed Pacifics, Nos 2750 and 4474 were transferred to Doncaster.

Another move which took place a little earlier

50
'B2' 4-6-0 No 5423 *Sir Sam Fay* enters Peterborough North with an express from Grimsby in 1937. *E. Neve*

51
'W1' 4-6-2-2 No 10000 takes water from Langley troughs as it speeds north with a down Leeds train on 20 April 1938.
E. R. Wethersett/Ian Allan Library

52
New 'A4' 4-6-2 No 4488, with its *Union of South Africa* nameplates covered prior to the official naming ceremony, with the 10.50 down Peterborough slow near Cemetery box in June 1937. *E. Neve*

53
Not on ex-GN metals! Two 'C1' 4-4-2s, Nos 4402/42, on the 16.10 slow train from Cambridge to Kings Cross at Trumpington on 16 April 1938.
E. R. Wethersett/Ian Allan Library

54
Mill Hill (The Hale) on 5 March 1938. 'N2' 0-6-2T No 4761 with a Finchley (Church End)-Edgware train.
E. R. Wethersett/Ian Allan Library

55
Langley, 20 April 1938. 'C12' 4-4-2T No 4511 deputising for a Sentinel railcar on a Hertford North to Letchworth train — one Gresley non-corridor coach and a Gresley GNR brake. *E. R. Wethersett/Ian Allan Library*

56
GNR Stirling Single No 1 with the set of ex-ECJS six-wheelers representing the 'Flying Scotsman' of 1888. Brookmans Park, 30 June 1938.
E. R. Wethersett/Ian Allan Library

was the transfer of 'A1' Pacifics Nos 2553/5 from Doncaster to Copley Hill for use on their Pullman diagrams to London. This meant eclipse of Ivatt Atlantics after almost 13 years of excellent service on Pullman duties. For use when one Pacific was not available Atlantic No 3280 was maintained in top condition thereby making occasional appearances.

GN 0-6-0STs seldom made news since their role was shunting and local trip goods duties. Hornsey shed had a North London Link which included trips to Poplar and Victoria Docks via Canonbury, Dalston and Victoria Park. One regular engine in this link was No 4252 and its two crews maintained it in spotless condition thereby earning the nick-name 'Pride of Hornsey'.

A full year's experience in operating the 'Silver Jubilee' train convinced the LNER management that more streamlined high-speed services should be put in hand. Operating costs of the Newcastle train were 2s 6d ($12\frac{1}{2}$p) per mile whilst receipts were 13s 11d ($69\frac{1}{2}$p). The supplementary fares charged had brought in £12,000 which represented 35% of the first cost of the train. It was decided to promote two new services in 1937 firstly to Edinburgh and later one to Leeds and Bradford.

Five new 'A4' Pacifics were built for use on the London-Edinburgh streamlined train which was named 'Coronation' and had a nine-car formation weighing 312ton empty as compared with 220ton of the 'Silver Jubilee'. The rear vehicle was an observation car shaped as a 'beaver tail', thus reversing the wedge shaped front of the locomotives and designed to reduce air resistance at the rear of the train. A unique exterior livery in two shades of blue, light for the upper panels and a darker garter blue for the lower panels. To match this the five locomotives were also turned out in garter blue, lined red and white, with dark red wheels and cut-out stainless steel numerals and lettering. The whole ensemble presented a fine spectacle. The five 'A4s' selected were Nos 4488-92 all named after British Dominions overseas and carried the coats of arms of those countries on the cab side sheets. Initially these five were allocated to Kings Cross Nos 4489/90/2; Haymarket Nos 4488/91. No 4492 was sent to Haymarket in July 1937.

The Press trip of the new train took place on Wednesday 30 June 1937 from Kings Cross to Barkston and back using No 4489 driven by G. Burfoot. No spectacular speeds were attempted on the down run accomplished in $93\frac{1}{2}$min. Because the LMSR had attained a maximum speed of 114mile/h on the Press run of their new 'Coronation Scot' train two days earlier, it was decided to try and beat that record on the return from Barkston. In fact only $109\frac{1}{2}$mile/h was achieved but with 92ton greater load.

Monday 5 July saw the new train enter service, departing from Kings Cross at 16.00 and Edinburgh at 16.30 to a level six-hour schedule. Going down the only stop was at York, 188.2 miles in 157min (71.9mile/h average). After a 3min break the 204.7mile run non-stop to Edinburgh was allowed 200min. Southbound the only intermediate call was at Newcastle (18.30 to 18.33). Thence 237min were allowed for the 268.4 miles to London, reached at 22.30. Not many regular observers were able to witness departure of the first down 'Coronation', taken by No 4491 and driver T. Dron (Gateshead) who, on the first ever occasion he had worked a high-speed regular train, put up a magnificent performance by reaching York $1\frac{1}{2}$min early. In the reverse direction driver G. Burfoot (Kings Cross) was less fortunate, having lost 2min by checks. On that memorable day many observers went to Euston to see the first up 'Coronation Scot' arrive punctually at 20.00 before moving along to Kings Cross to await arrival of 'Coronation'.

For the summer of 1937 the schedule of the non-stop 'Flying Scotsman' came down to 7hr each way between London and Edinburgh with 'A4' haulage. To make this change possible corridor tenders were removed from the 'A1' and 'A3' Pacifics and attached to 'A4s', and new 'A4s' Nos 4491-7 all had corridor tenders when built, like Nos 2509-12. The last 'A3' to run with a corridor tender was No 2750 *Papyrus* which did some work on the 1937 non-stop before the tender was changed.

Two notable records were made by Haymarket shed by keeping No 4491 on the 'Coronation' for 48 out of the first 51 runs of that train on which a total of 18,864 miles were covered at high speed and a further 4,323 on the Sunday working. At the same time No 4492 made 52 consecutive runs on the 'Flying Scotsman' totalling 20,436 miles of which 14,394 were made non-stop between Edinburgh and London, 3,144 on the Saturday train making one stop, at Newcastle, and 2,538 on Sunday balancing trains.

Only Kings Cross and Haymarket engines were rostered for the 'Coronation', going through each way with a crew change at York northbound and Newcastle southbound. Balancing Sunday trains were 18.00 Kings Cross-Newcastle, after which the engine was worked forward to Edinburgh and 17.20 Newcastle-London arrive 22.45. For the first few months crews changed at York northbound but when a Newcastle stop was inserted in March 1938 the change was made there.

To accommodate the additional lodging turn two extra crews were added to Top Shed's No 1 link, making a total of 10 crews and Gateshead No 1 link had seven crews, reduced to six in March 1938 when they ceased to work the 'Coronation' from York to Edinburgh. At that time the six drivers had regular booked engines — all 'A4' Nos 4462 (driver Morton), 4463 (Ferguson), 4465 (Coates), 4499 (Waite), 4500 (Nicholson) and 4901 (Hannah). In the six-week roster there were four lodge turns to London and one weekday out and home trip each to Edinburgh and Leeds thereby giving Gateshead crews the most extensive route knowledge of any East Coast men.

The third LNER streamliner, named 'West Riding Limited' went into service on 27 September 1937 using a set train identical with 'Coronation' but without a 'Beaver Tail'. Departure from Kings Cross was at 19.10 and Leeds reached at 21.53. Reversal took place at Leeds whence the train was taken on to Bradford by a pair of 'N2' 0-6-2T arriving at 22.15. In the opposite direction the train started from Bradford at 11.10 and with similar arrangements as for the down working, left Leeds at 11.33 on its non-stop dash to London. From Doncaster it followed 15min behind the 'Silver Jubilee' to reach Kings Cross at 14.15. Two 'A4s' Nos 4495 *Golden Fleece* and 4496 *Golden Shuttle* were allocated to Top Shed for the duty.

All locomotive duties for the 'West Riding Limited' were undertaken by Kings Cross shed where there was a revival of a No 1A Link of six crews as previously the case with the Pullman Link of 1926-35. The men came from No 2 Link (4) and No 3 (Express Goods-2), none having previous experience of high-speed running. As with the other streamlined trains the 'West Riding Limited' ran on Mondays to Fridays only. For Monday's southbound working engine and men took the 18.10 ordinary express to Leeds on Sunday and subsequently the 19.10 northbound service on Tuesday and Thursday. The second set worked the 19.10 Monday, Wednesday and Friday to return with the 11.33 from Leeds on Tuesday and Thursday. Their return to London on Saturday was with the leisurely 12.35 Leeds-London which took two minutes under four hours for the journey in distinct contrast to the 2hr 43min of the streamliner. The other four turns in No 1A link were on slow or semi-fast trains to Grantham and Peterborough and on three days per week to Cambridge on the 9.35 'Buffet Express', together with one week on the main line pilot duty.

After rebuilding at Doncaster with a conventional boiler and streamlined exterior like the 'A4' class, the erstwhile 'Hush-Hush' engine No 10000 was allocated to Top Shed early in November 1937. Following 10 days on customary running-in turns, mostly to Peterborough, the 4-6-4 went to work in the Newcastle link turn about with 'A4s'. A unique feature of this rebuild was the provision of electric lighting beneath the valances to illuminate the driving wheels and motion during hours of darkness. Lineside observers in the suburbs were fascinated by this new idea, seen to advantage when the engine worked up on the 'Afternoon Scotsman' due Kings Cross at 21.35. In February 1938 the 'W1' was transferred to Doncaster for use on the 11.04 from there, due into London at 13.47 and the 16.00 return. The latter was always a heavy formation and from the introduction of the 16.00 'Coronation' it travelled on the slow line to Finsbury Park No 5 box where it was turned on to the fast line to follow the streamline train. When the 16.00 working became part of a cyclic diagram in 1939, No 10000 returned to Kings Cross but was never used on high-speed trains except on two occasions. The first of these was on 4 January 1939 when it replaced 'A4' No 4482 at Grantham on the down 'Coronation' but failed at Durham where Class G5 0-4-4T No 1837 took over to Newcastle. Secondly, on Sunday 22 July 1939 the 4-6-4 was provided to take the 12.40 Newcastle in order to return south on the 'Silver Jubilee' next morning. On this occasion the streamline train reached Kings Cross on time, capably handled by driver W. Sheen.

Several excursions were run from Scotland to London for the International Football match at Wembley on 9 April 1938 when four Haymarket

57
'A1' 4-6-2 No 2555 *Centenary* eases the up 'Queen of Scots' Pullman through Peterborough North in 1938. *E. Neve collection*

58
'A4' 4-6-2 No 4468 *Mallard* on its way to everlasting fame with the test train of 3 July 1938. Passing Potters Bar. *L. J. Burley*

59
A rare picture. 'C1' 4-4-2 No 3290 passes New Barnet southbound with the return of the test train stock including dynamometer car on 3 July 1938, the occasion of *Mallard*'s record-breaking run. No 3290, Peterborough's main line pilot, had replaced No 4468 at Peterborough. *L. J. Burley*

60
Kings Cross (Metropolitan) old station on 24 August 1938. 'N2' 0-6-2T No 4757 with a Moorgate-Alexandra Palace train. *H. C. Casserley*

61
With Driver Duddington at the regulator, 'A3' 4-6-2 No 4477 *Gay Crusader* heading the up 'Yorkshire Pullman' through Harringay. *Real Photos*

62
The Peterborough North pilot — 'C12' 4-4-2T No 4540 waiting to attach a buffet car, converted from a GNR open third, to an up express. August 1938. *E. Neve*

63
'K3' 2-6-0 No 2455 runs slowly through Peterborough North with a southbound No 1 express goods in 1938. Atlantic pilot in the background. *E. Neve*

'A4s', Nos 4483/4/91/7 came through to Kings Cross and returned later the same day.

Grantham shed received its first 'A4s' in May 1938 for use on a new diagram (SX) on which the engines travelled through from Grantham to Edinburgh.

A severe snowstorm on Wednesday 25 January 1939 caused complete breakdown of communications in the London Area. Three trains were in collision just north of Hatfield station where the up 'Aberdonian' had been standing at No 2 box with two trains from Cambridge behind it. Around 10.00 this queue was run into by the 7.15 ex-Peterborough semi-fast hauled by 'V2' No 4813. One person was killed in the collision which blocked all lines for many hours. Lack of telephones meant the news did not reach Wood Green until 11.15. Meanwhile down trains had been sent forward at caution but were stopped south of Hatfield. The 10.00 'Flying Scotsman' and 10.15 West Riding expresses were reversed and returned to Wood Green where they did not arrive until after 13.00 to reverse once more and proceed via Cuffley and Hertford to Langley Jct to rejoin the main line. The first train diverted directly at Wood Green was the 11.20 'Queen of Scots' Pullman and the following 11.30 York semi-fast stalled on the flyover. All trains in either direction stopped at Palmers Green for instructions to proceed. Here, later in the day the 16.00 down 'Coronation' was seen at 16.35 behind 'A4' No 4493; the 'Silver Jubilee' was made up of ordinary stock behind 'A4' No 4498 at 18.25, followed by No 4901 on the 17.45 Newcastle whilst No 4496 on the 'West Riding Ltd' arrived at 19.43. Southbound trains were more heavily delayed. The 'West Riding Ltd', did not appear until 16.18 (No 4496); the 'Yorkshire Pullman' at 18.06 (No 2744), followed quickly by No 4474 on an excursion which was probably due into London at 14.30.

In March 1939 the last Pullman special to Aintree for the Grand National was taken by No 2561 *Minoru* which engine had taken the first such train from Kings Cross in 1929.

Apart from the appearance of 'V2' 2-6-2s on Newmarket Race trains for the first time in 1938, interest was aroused by the use of Top Shed Pacifics on the 9.35 Cambridge Buffet Express and 12.30 return. This was occasioned by greatly increased patronage of the up train on which half-day cheap fares were available on Thursdays and Saturdays. The load of these trains rose to 10 or 12 bogies which was beyond the capacity of Ivatt Atlantics to work punctually. In addition to 'A4s' use was made of 'A1', 'V2' and on four occasions even No 10000.

A number of cyclic engine diagrams were introduced in March 1939 causing some redistribution of Pacifics. Top shed lost their famous No 4472 to Doncaster but received two 'A3s' Nos 2504 and 4480 in exchange whilst another well-known Kings Cross Pacific No 2750 moved to Grantham. A start was also made in transferring 'A1s' to the Great Central Section which received Nos 4473/4/8, 2546/52/4/8/62 during the year. In addition Doncaster lost 'A3' No 2544 *Lemberg* to Gateshead and the Scottish Area 'A1' No 2556 whilst Grantham sent 'A1' No 2559 to Gateshead. Several of the new diagrams meant that Kings Cross engines alternated with Gateshead on duties such as 16.00 Kings Cross-Newcastle M/W/F; 1-14 Newcastle-Edinburgh; 8.05 Edinburgh-Doncaster Tu-Th-S and finally 23.50 Doncaster-Kings Cross. The London 'A4' for for down West Riding first worked to Doncaster at 7.25 from Kings Cross whence it arrived back at 15.47 and then took the 19.10 streamlined 'West Riding Ltd' to Leeds. The Grantham 'A4' diagram started from there at 12.18 stopping train to Doncaster; 16.10 (ex-Leeds) express to Kings Cross arrive 18.55; 22.25 sleeping car train Kings Cross-Newcastle arrive 4.20; 18.35 Newcastle-Edinburgh and 23.00 Edinburgh-Grantham arrive 5.02. This diagram required two engines weekly. In all cases crews changed at various points en route.

During the peak summer service Doncaster shed was short of Pacifics to cover their weekday diagrams and were obliged to use 'V2s' on the 'Yorkshire Pullman' to and from London on four consecutive days in July. Also in the summer the veteran Kings Cross 'A1' No 4475 *Flying Fox* put up a notable performance by running on Newcastle through turns for 15 weeks and 'A4' No 4489 *Dominion of Canada* completed 34 consecutive trips on the non-stop 'Flying Scotsman' to Edinburgh, followed by one week on the 'Coronation', then four more weeks on the non-stop and one further week on the 'Flying Scotsman' when it made only one intermediate call, at Newcastle.

In those four glorious years between September 1935 and August 1939 the GN line recorders had plenty to do in compiling daily lists of train workings. Naturally the three streamlined trains were the principal target. Obviously no single person could ever hope to see every train so a schedule developed whereby those working near the main line could adjust their lunch times to cover the up 'Silver Jubilee' and 'West Riding Ltd' and one whose place of business was close to Kings Cross was able to see the 'Coronation' depart at 16.00. Less difficulty arose over the northbound 17.30 and 19.10 departures to Newcastle and Leeds/Bradford. For some living close to the line a nightly ritual developed to meet soon after 22.00 to witness 'Coronation's swift passage through the suburbs. On Friday nights the regulars often congregated at Oakleigh Park and were joined by homegoing travellers arriving on the local train at 22.11. The impressive scene was enlivened on those occasions when the driver was A. J. Taylor, OBE who lived near Oakleigh Park station and always sounded two long blasts on the chime whistle to tell his wife he would be home for supper at 23.15!

Two completely new trains were built in 1938 for the 'Flying Scotsman'. Maximum publicity was given to these fine coaches on 30 June when a demonstration was staged to illustrate progress made over 50 years. For this purpose a rake of seven GNR six wheeled low roof vehicles was restored to ECJS livery and the famous Stirling 8ft Single, No 1 taken out of York Museum and put into working order to haul them. On the demonstration run privileged guests were taken from Kings Cross to Stevenage in the old train, depicting the 'Flying Scotsman' of 1888. At Stevenage the occupants transferred to the new set of coaches, hauled by 'A4' No 4498 *Sir Nigel Gresley* for the next stage down to Barkston. Using the triangular junctions at Barkston the train was reversed and by an inspired piece of organisation the passengers were treated to a broadside view of 'Coronation' speeding northwards to Edinburgh, after which the train returned to Kings Cross.

The trouble and expense incurred in restoring the old train was put to good use later when it travelled to various parts of the LNER system giving special trips. Two of these were from Kings Cross. The first on 24 August conveyed passengers to Cambridge and back.

Departing at 11.04 the first stop was at Hitchin to take water and Cambridge was reached at $12.42\frac{1}{2}$. Return from Cambridge was at 18.35 and arrival in Kings Cross 20.14 where it was noticed some participants had dressed in 1888 period costume.

The event inspired officers of the Railway Correspondence and Travel Society to charter the train for their members on Sunday 11 September when Peterborough was the destination. Thus the ordinary enthusiast gained an opportunity, undreamed of before, to travel behind one of the most famous British locomotives. Everyone had a most memorable outing and photographers had an unprecedented field day.

In July 1938 the last 'A4' emerged from Doncaster, numbered 4903 and named *Peregrine* it was allocated to Kings Cross. The complete 'A4' allocation then was: Kings Cross Nos 2509/10/12, 4467/89/92/3/5/6/8, 4902/3 – 12; Grantham Nos 4466/94 – 2; Doncaster Nos 4468, 4900 – 2; Gateshead Nos 2511, 4462/3/5/9, 4499, 4500, 4901 – 8; Heaton No 4464 – 1; Haymarket Nos 4482-8/90/1/7 – 10.

Description of the events of 3 July 1938 have received ample publicity. Suffice to say here that No 4468 *Mallard* was worked up to Kings Cross the previous day by driver Duddington from Doncaster. After the world speed record had been attained and *Mallard* removed from the train at Peterborough, the journey back to London was made by 'C1' No 3290. This was done to avoid any severe damage to the 'A4's' middle big-end from which the white metal had run out. Re-metalling was done at New England shed and after a thorough inspection at Doncaster Plant to ensure nothing else had been damaged the engine returned to its appointed place in the Doncaster link nine days after the event. These facts refute utterly stories put about in later years that the engine was 'completely smashed up'.

For most of us the threat of war caused a sudden drop in regular observation. On Thursday, 31 August 1939 the streamline era came to a close. The last 'Silver Jubilee' runs were by 'A4s' Nos 4489 (up) and 4499 (down); 'Coronation' 4487 (down) and 4488 (up); 'West Riding Ltd' 4495 (up) and 4496 (down). Although we did not know at the time these magnificent trains would never return to the East Coast Route.

In the emergency timetable of September 1939 there were but three trains to Edinburgh weekdays, taking from 8hr 25min to 9hr 40min. (In the previous timetable there had been 17 day trains to

Edinburgh averaging 7hr 31min on Saturdays). To the West Riding where were five trains and one to Hull. This severe reduction meant there were many more passenger locomotives than could be used. It was stated the Kings Cross 'A4s' were put into store but this is difficult to substantiate.

New hazards soon presented themselves to railway operators. On 25 November 1939 all trains were delayed after 16.30 when a barrage balloon stationed in the waterworks at Wood Green dragged its lorry into the New River, lost height and pulled the cable across all running lines.

Work commenced late in November on re-instating the spur at Harringay to join the Tottenham & Hampstead line. This spur was originally put in during World War 1 but removed later. Engineers trains hauled by GN 'J1' 0-6-0 No 3010 and an unidentified GE 0-6-0T were seen there on 26 November.

64
With bell ringing, 'A4' 4-6-2 No 4489 *Dominion of Canada* eases up the non-stop 'Flying Scotsman' through Peterborough North in 1938. *E. Neve*

65
The up 'Junior Scotsman' at Peterborough North in 1938, with 'A4' 4-6-2 No 4903 *Peregrine* at its head. *E. Neve*

66
'V2' 2-6-2 No 4798 brings the 7.08 ex-Leeds 'Party' train into Potters Bar in August 1938. Note all-steel bogie van behind the engine. *E. Neve*

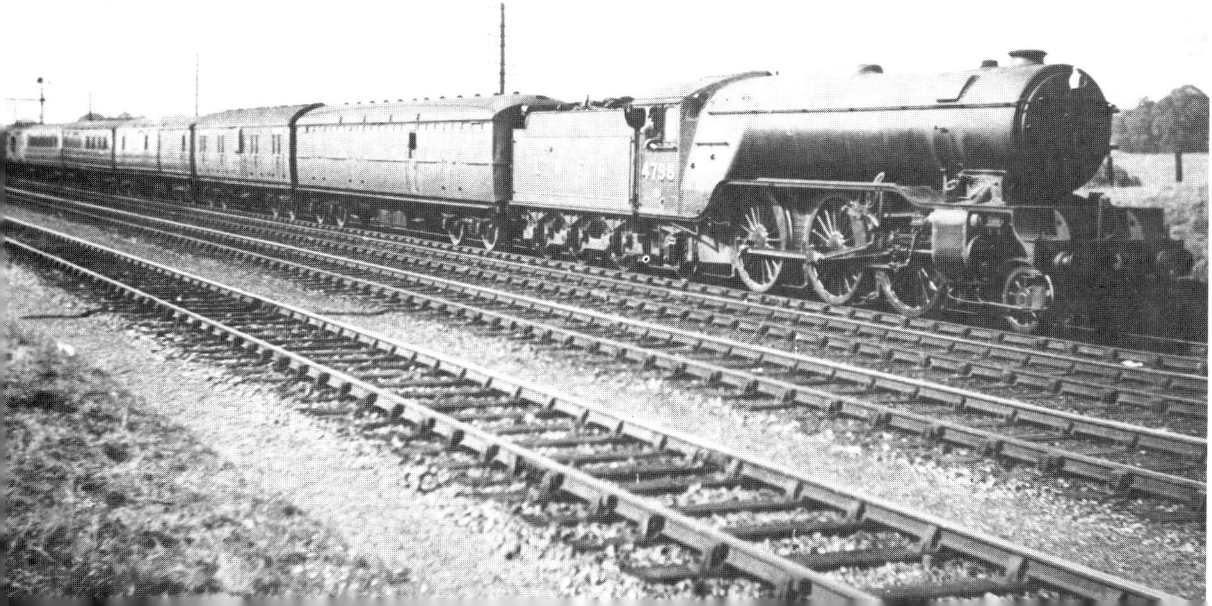

67
'A4' 4-6-2 No 4494 *Osprey* in green livery approaches Potters Bar with an up express in August 1938. *E. Neve*

68
'A4' 4-6-2 No 4495 *Golden Fleece* on Werrington troughs with the new 'Flying Scotsman' train set on 4 July 1938. *T. G. Hepburn/Rail Archive Stephenson*

69
An up goods at Corby Glen in July 1939 with 'K3' 2-6-0 No 4002. *H. Gordon Tidey*

1940-1947

For most railway enthusiasts the coming of war meant almost total cessation of their interests. In the early days when the situation was uncertain, putting nerves on edge, it was most unwise to be seen taking notes and severe reduction in all train services together with blackout conditions did not offer much encouragement to observers.

An Emergency Timetable came into force on Sunday 10 September 1939 providing drastically reduced services to all destinations. Only four trains left Kings Cross for Scotland at 10.00, 13.00, 19.00 and 22.15 all terminating at Edinburgh. Yorkshire departures were at 10.20, 13.15, and 16.00. The last had through coaches to Newcastle as previously. This meagre service proved quite inadequate making relief trains a regular necessity. In December additional trains were put on at 9.50, 12.30 and 17.00 for Newcastle. The 20.25 Edinburgh was restored and the 7.25 Leeds whilst Hull was served by a new 17.55 departure. Similar arrangements applied in the opposite direction.

Significant changes in suburban trains were also apparent. Not only were frequencies curtailed but all locals except those between Kings Cross and Hatfield operated only to or from Finsbury Park. Both Broad Street and Moorgate trains were

suspended as were Finchley-Edgware and Hitchin-Hertford North. Improvements were made from 4 December when Kings Cross resumed handling local trains once more and a much reduced Broad Street service was restored. Moorgate trains were not restored until 1 January 1940, restricted to a few morning arrivals until 4 August when four evening departures to East Finchley were introduced. Subsequently frequent interruptions were caused by heavy bombing raids which were directly responsible for the sudden withdrawal of all Broad Street trains from 4 October. Thus ended an unusual working arrangement spanning 65 years.

Prior to withdrawal LMS engines remained in use on the GN trains to Broad Street but hauling standard GN eight-coach articulated sets as on 5 February 1940 when the 17.11 Broad Street-High Barnet had LMS 0-6-0T No 7498 bunker first hauling set No 91 and on 2 March the 13.57 Broad Street-Gordon Hill was taken by 2-6-2T No 82 plus set 59. Certain LMS engines were also operating between Finsbury Park and GN line destinations.

Steam hauled local trains to High Barnet ceased on 13 April 1940 when the last working was taken by 'N2' No 4750. Next morning London Transport Tube trains commenced running through from Highgate Archway to East Finchley and High Barnet. Whilst Highgate (LNE) station was being rebuilt to accommodate tube trains the LNER operated a steam service of 40 weekday and 16 Sunday trains to East Finchley. Most were to or from Finsbury Park only but a few ran between Kings Cross or Moorgate and East Finchley. Loss of the High Barnet workings plus reduced services on other lines enabled a number of 'N2' 0-6-2Ts to be transferred to provincial centres, several going to Mexborough where they were used to bank heavy goods or mineral trains from Wath to Dunford Bridge.

The severe reductions in main line services gave rise to exceptionally heavy loads and 20-coach for-

70
Thompson 'A1/1' 4-6-2 No 4470 *Great Northern* at Potters Bar summit with the 16.50 Kings Cross-Peterborough in 1947. *Derrick A. Dant*

mations became commonplace. Gresley's big engine policy paid handsome dividends at this time when his Pacifics and 'Green Arrows' were able to handle these huge formations without assistance. As the Kings Cross arrival platforms could not accommodate such lengthy trains the procedure was for an 'N2' 0-6-2T to follow the incoming train from Belle Isle at caution and then draw off the rear five or six coaches which were placed in another platform.

Three notable events illustrating the handling of exceptional loads may be quoted: On Sunday 31 March 1940 the 10.45 to London left Newcastle with 16 coaches (518ton) in showery, windy weather and headed by Gateshead's famous 'A1' Pacific No 2569 *Gladiateur*. Eleven minutes were spent at Darlington where three more coaches were added, bringing the load up to 603ton gross. The 44.1 miles on to York took 52min and there the load was increased by another three coaches, making 22 in all (664ton). Only 3min were debited against the engine to the next stop at Doncaster and after calls at Retford, Newark and Grantham, where it was necessary to draw up each time, Peterborough was reached 83min late, of which eight had been set against the engine. During a 13min stop at Peterborough No 2569 was detached and a further two coaches and two fish vans were added to the already colossal load which then amounted to 764ton gross. Leaving Peterborough at 16.57 with engine No 4800 ('V2') the New England crew covered the 76.4 miles to Kings Cross in 102min of which nine were lost by the engine but one may reasonably ask where else in the British Isles would so great a load have been tackled unaided by one engine and crew? The 268-mile journey from Newcastle to London had taken all but eight hours. A few months previously it took only 5hr 5min.

Two other remarkable events occurred on Friday 5 April 1940 when the 13.00 Edinburgh express left Kings Cross with no less than 25 coaches headed by the pioneer 'A4' No 2509 *Silver Link*. The front coaches had to be loaded in a separate platform, drawn into Gasworks tunnel and backed on to the main train. Thus the engine and some coaches were well inside the tunnel and the starting signal was conveyed to the driver by ground staff. It took 16min for this huge load, computed at 850ton gross, to surmount the difficult 1 in 105/110 bank out to Finsbury Park ($2\frac{1}{2}$ miles). After this initial climb the ensuing 103 miles to Grantham were run in 123min against 112 allowed but credit was due to Grantham driver W. Carman and his fireman in getting such a train out of Kings Cross without stalling. After changing crews at Grantham and York No 2509 continued through to Newcastle losing only 4min over the 163 miles.

Later the same day the 13.55 ex-Leeds left Peterborough with a 24 coach load weighing 759ton tare which another Grantham driver and 'A1' No 2549 *Persimmon* succeeded in hauling to Kings Cross in 96min on a 94min schedule averaging 47.8mile/h.

Further timetable revisions were made on 15 May 1940 when there were 13 express and four semi-fast or stopping trains each weekday out of Kings Cross compared with 25 and 10 respectively in 1939. It is worth recalling that on Saturdays in July/August 1930 17 day trains left Kings Cross for Edinburgh or beyond, averaging 7hr 31min over the $392\frac{3}{4}$ miles which was taking around nine hours in 1940. At this time the restored 16.05 Cleethorpes express was often hauled by 'B17' 'Sandringham' 4-6-0s Nos 2849/51 which spent a brief period working from New England shed on duties to both London and Grimsby.

Many new features became apparent to those still able to observe events. When an air raid warning was sounded, trains were stopped by signal for the special air raid head code to be applied — one lamp in the centre of the buffer beam. At first maximum speeds during warning periods were fixed at 15mile/h for passenger and 10 for goods, increased from 11 November 1940 to 25 and 15 respectively to apply in the blackout only. To assist shunters in the night hours some 0-6-0STs had bufferbeams painted white at least one 'N1' 0-6-2T was similarly treated.

To facilitate cross-London journeys and enable greater loads to be conveyed by Ferme Park-Feltham transfer trips, four daily trains were scheduled to use the newly restored spur at Harringay from the GN to the Tottenham & Hampstead line. For these duties six GE 0-6-0s of Class J17 numbered 8164/84, 8204/8/35/6 were transferred to Hornsey. Thirty-six loaded wagons were permitted and 50 empty on the return trips made via Canonbury. In addition to the 'J17' engines 'O1' Nos 3463/72/4 and 'J52' Nos 4204/16/34 were also seen.

On main line goods duties some GC 'O4' 2-8-0s had returned to New England after an interval of five years and a new class for the district was represented by 'J39' 0-6-0s Nos 1952 and 2982 working regularly to Hornsey for the first time. An unusual combination seen in May 1940 taking the Ashburton Grove refuse train through Finsbury Park was 'O4' No 6321 and 'J17' 8236.

Surprisingly, in view of prevailing conditions, a race special from Newmarket was seen on 13 June 1940 in charge of 'A1' Pacific No 4476 which soon after was transferred to New England shed from Kings Cross along with Nos 4475 and 2561. Initially the first allocation of Pacifics to Peterborough was to cover duties involving the 10.0 ex-Kings Cross as far as York and the new Colchester-Leeds and Colchester-Edinburgh through trains northwards from Peterborough. Exactly what additional duties devolved upon New England shed are not known but in October 1942 they received three more Pacifics, Nos 2549/53/60 and just prior to 'D Day' (June 1944) a further seven were allocated there for varying periods.

Like many other railways near London the GN lines experienced much damage by enemy action from 9 September 1940 onwards. On that day there were no trains to Broad Street or Moorgate following heavy raids and on 27th no trains operated south of Wood Green where both main line and local services started or terminated. At 17.30 Waterworks sidings contained several Pacifics and 'V2s'. 'A3' No 2744 arrived about three hours late with the 10.15 ex-Leeds and then 'C1' No 3295 entered the up fast platform with a bogie local set to which another Atlantic No 4434 was coupled at the rear forming the 17.10 Baldock slow. From Waterworks sidings 'A4' No 4495 crossed over to Hornsey carriage sidings to collect a 15-coach rake which it worked forward over the long cross-over into No 1 down slow platform at Wood Green to form the 17.25 Newcastle, leaving at 18.00. Another 'A4', No 4468 was in Bounds Green sidings after bringing an express from the north. Normal main line services resumed next day and Broad Street three days later. On Saturday 5 October 1940 bombs fell on the down goods line between Wood Green station and tunnel box west of the Hertford line fly-over which suffered some damage. The goods line, known to railwaymen as the 'Khyber Pass' remained blocked but the fly-over was soon repaired for use next day. Delayed action bombs close to the line near Enfield Chase station caused all trains to be diverted into the disused Enfield Old platforms on 12 October. Buses conveyed passengers beyond Enfield for six days until the danger was removed. About noon on Sunday 3 November bombs fell near Hornsey station demolishing the footbridge and blocking several running lines.

On the night of 10 May 1941 when much damage was done in the vicinity, Kings Cross received a direct hit on the offices beside No 10 platform and 'N2' 0-6-2T No 4759 was damaged in this incident. Trains used the eastern half of the station until normal working was restored.

On the locomotive front arrival of newly built 'V2' 2-6-2s was evident and in October 1941 Tyneside Pacifics and 'V2s' began to reach Kings Cross at 16.10 on weekdays. These engines had not worked south of Peterborough on diagrammed duties since September 1939.

In March 1942 as an economy measure all locomotives began to appear in unlined black livery. Early examples noted were 'A1' No 4475 *Flying Fox* and 'A4' 2512 *Silver Fox*.

At this time some regular observation revealed the unique 4-6-4 No 10000 often taking the 13.10 Leeds express from Kings Cross. From May to August it was regularly on the night sleeper train due at 7.35. Unusually a Mexborough based engine, 'V2' No 4877, took the 16.00 to Leeds on 17 June.

Tyneside engines seen were Gateshead 'V2' No 4897 arriving at 18.35 on 15 August and No 2579 *Dick Turpin* of Heaton brought in the 10.52 arrival from Grantham on 21 August. Although most Cambridge duties to Kings Cross had 'C1' Atlantics or 'B17' Sandringhams' a 'B12/3' No 8514 was observed several times arriving at 17.18 and going back at 19.50.

A timetable revision on 15 October 1942 brought a surprising weekday through working of a Doncaster large Atlantic to London. Leaving Doncaster at 7.42 on a stopping train which called all stations to Hitchin, then Finsbury Park to reach Kings Cross at 14.42. Return was on the 22.25 Leeds express due into Doncaster at 1.11. This was the first regularly diagrammed Atlantic duty from Doncaster to London since Grouping. It lasted for about one year. The sight of well groomed Atlantics from so far away was a cheering sight at such a gloomy time.

The Alexandra Palace local train service was changed to pull and push working operating from Finsbury Park from 7 September 1942. Auto fitted Class F2 2-4-2T Nos 5777/8/83 of GCR origin were first used and the class continued to operate the service until replaced in 1950. When one of the three engines was not available an 'N2' 0-6-2T was used but had to run round the two coaches each end of the journey.

Because loads of express trains were still ranging from 16 to 20 coaches, permission was given for tank engines, which had worked the empty stock into Kings Cross, to give banking assistance when the load exceeded 16 vehicles. Usually the banker dropped off when reaching the centre footbridge. To obtain assistance train engine drivers had to give three crows on their whistle which could be most entertaining on an 'A4' chime!

Back in April 1941 the sudden death of Sir Nigel Gresley had saddened every GN line enthusiast and many enginemen as well, some of whom were not slow to recall occasions when he had ridden behind them and never failed to speak to them afterwards. Speculation as to future developments were rife but the first signs did not come until 31 March 1943 when the rebuilt 'P2' 2-8-2 No 2005, now in the form of a Pacific classed 'A2', reached Kings Cross with a Leeds express due at 14.46 and returned to Doncaster at 16.00. The engine was not again seen in London for some years.

Coal traffic to and via London had increased steadily as war progressed due partly to reductions in coastal seaborne traffic and to some rerouting away from the GE lines which were carrying heavy traffic for the many airfields and other military establishments in East Anglia. The Gresley two and three-cylinder 2-8-0s of Classes 01 and 02 had put in 20-30 years of hard slogging on the New England-Ferme Park (Hornsey) coal trains and were in 1943 showing signs of wear. They had received assistance from GC 04 and Gresley 'K3' 2-6-0s, neither or which could haul the same loads as the Gresley 2-8-0s. It was with relief that the operating authorities recieved a number of newly built Ministry of Supply 'Austerity' 2-8-0s on loan pending their shipment to Europe in 1944. In mid-April 1943 the first examples, Nos 7008/22, 7300 were all noted at New Southgate on coal trains. Eventually eight weekday fast unbraked coal/empties were introduced between New England and Hornsey conveying 60 loaded and 70 empty wagons with 20ton brake vans. The schedules were just under three hours in either direction. Enginemen worked out and home return trips on these duties, as had been done prewar but the work was now shared between New England (five trips) and Hornsey (three trips). On Sundays there were three southbound loaded trains and four northbound empty wagon trains.

Through engine workings from Leeds were introduced in October 1943 when three 'A1' Pacifics, Nos 2545/51/4 were transferred to Copley Hill shed from Grantham which received three 'A4' Nos 4467/8, 4900 from Doncaster.

In the autumn of 1943 details of some links at Kings Cross Top Shed became available to me. By then the erstwhile prewar links Nos 1, 1A/2/3/4 had been reduced to only two of which No 1 comprised 19 crews working mainly passenger train duties to Grantham (9), Peterborough (6), Cambridge (2) and two main line pilot turns. No 2 link had 29 crews who covered only eight passenger train duties to Hitchin (3), Baldock (1), Royston (1), Cambridge (2) and Peterborough (1). The remaining duties were very complex involving braked goods and fish empties to Peterborough plus some parcels trains and empty wagons from Ferme Park northwards. Of the prewar No 1 link only four drivers remained in service but five of the six from No 1A were still active. These men, who in 1939, had been working streamlined express trains to Newcastle and Leeds were now engaged in some menial duties indeed.

At Grantham the Top link was still very similar to prewar. Still having 10 crews working six expresses to London and back, two to York, one to Lincoln to maintain route knowledge in case of diversion and one pilot turn.

A southbound goods was derailed at Arlesey in the early hours of Saturday, 2 October 1943, blocking both running lines. All trains were diverted at Hitchin to travel via Cambridge and March to Peterborough. Heavy delays were experienced. The sleeping car train from Edinburgh due into Kings Cross at 7.10 arrived at noon in charge of 'K2' 2-6-0 No 4656 (March) hauling 20 coaches. It was followed by 'V2' No 4871 on the 'Aberdonian'. The 4.15 from Kings Cross to Leeds was taken through from Cambridge to Grantham by former 'Royal' 'Claud Hamilton' 4-4-0 No 8787 which made very heavy weather over the 29.1 miles from Peterborough to Grantham with a Grantham crew.

In July 1943 came news of the withdrawal of Ivatt large Atlantic No 4459 (Kings Cross), the first standard 'C1' to go. Over many years No 4459 had been one of Top Shed's star performers. Although these old engines were still performing well on a variety of duties their condition was rapidly declining under wartime difficulties.

An unusual accident occurred at Kings Cross on 7 July 1943 when the 12.37 ex-Hertford local train was entering platform 14 the engine jumped off the rails on a crossing in the yard. Although all wheels were derailed little damage was done due to slow speed. By 16.00 No 2682 (Class N2) had been re-railed.

Next evening 'A4' No 2509 *Silver Link* on the 20.20 Edinburgh Mail was stopped at Wood Green after two coupling rods had fractured. The pilot engine was summoned from Kings Cross to replace No 2509 and the train finally left Wood Green at 21.10 in charge of 'A1' No 2558.

What is believed to be the first use of an 'Austerity' 2-8-0 on an express passenger train into Kings Cross took place on 11 January 1944 when the 10.15 ex-Leeds, due at 14.46 did not arrive until 16.20 behind No 7084 which had been attached at Offord after failure of the train engine.

A totally new feature was introduced from 7 February 1944 when the stopping passenger trains leaving Peterborough at 9.35 and 11.50 ran non-stop from Hitchin to Finsbury Park via Langley Jct, Hertford North and Wood Green. The first train reached London at 12.27 and the engine returned to Peterborough at 16.05 with the Cleethorpes express which often loaded to 13 coaches. For some time the rebuilt 'C1' No 3279 was employed on this duty.

On 11 April 1944 a surprising sight on the 17.55 Kings Cross-Peterborough stopping train was 'B2' 4-6-0 No 5425 *City of Manchester*.

In advance of final preparations for the invasion of Europe on 6 June 1944 drastic curtailment of all passenger train services took place. Seven trains in either direction at Kings Cross were suspended including the up 'Flying Scotsman' at 10.00 from Edinburgh. This meant the following 10.10 had to make additional stops en route on its 9hr 10min journey to London. The cuts were restored on 31 July. No through engines were diagrammed from north of Grantham into London at this time. There was an unusual duty for one of the 'F2' 2-4-2T which ran the empty stock forming the 15.21 to Cambridge into Kings Cross before running light to Finsbury Park to take up duty on the Alexandra Palace branch pull and push service.

Two derailments occurred at Wood Green in August 1944. On 21 August the engine and 10 coaches of the 16.00 Kings Cross-Leeds were derailed south of the station and a week later 'N2' No 2675 on the 17.21 Finsbury Park-Gordon Hill, first stop Bowes Park, took the turn-out to the flyover north of Wood Green platforms rather too fast and was overturned. Fortunately no serious casualties occurred in either incident.

The newly installed double line through running connection from the GE Section Palace Gates branch to the GN Hertford line at Bounds Green was put into full use. A number of trains were scheduled between Temple Mills and Peterborough or March via Hitchin with Stratford crews working to Hitchin.

Although much use was made of 'J39' 0-6-0s on these duties, other classes were seen including WD 2-8-0 'K2' and 'K3' and various GE 0-6-0.

In 1944 the first fruits of E. Thompson's locomotive policy began to appear on the GN lines. The first 'B1' 4-6-0 No 8301 *Springbok* took the 12.20 Kings Cross-Cambridge and 17.20 return on 13 and 15 June. Both trains stopped at all stations between Hatfield and Cambridge. On 23 June No 8301 undertook a Kings Cross No 1 link duty to Peterborough on the 7.23 slow, returning with the 8.40 ex-Cleethorpes express arriving in London at 13.15. Cambridge shed turned out another 'B1' No 8304 *Gazelle* for a Royal Train leaving Kings Cross at 15.00 to Wolferton on 28 September and used this engine for a time on their daily duty reaching Kings Cross at 17.20 and 19.50 return.

As all the 'Austerity' 2-8-0s had been called up by the War Department for shipment to Europe all GN Section coal and unbraked goods trains reverted to 'K3', 'O2' and 'O4' haulage with occasional use of 'J39' and even 'Q4' 0-8-0s. The special fast coal train schedules had to be abandoned.

In the autumn of 1944 the 47 year old Ivatt Class D3 4-4-0 No 4075 was overhauled at Doncaster and given a new side window cab. It was repainted in LNER green livery and the tender carried hand-painted LNER coats of arms on each side between the letters 'N E'. Although Thompson at first decided to allot the number 1 to this engine,

71
Suburban services were disrupted when a footbridge over the GN main line at Hornsey collapsed into a bomb crater. *BR*

72
Kings Cross station — the bar and grill room, Platform 10, have disappeared into rubble, 1941. *BR*

73
It was May 1941 before the censor approved publication of this photograph of 'O2' 2-8-0 No 3462 damaged during the September 1940 blitz. *BR*

74
Kings Cross shed, after bombing, September 1940. Visible are 'V2' 2-6-2s Nos 4883 (left) and 4797. *BR*

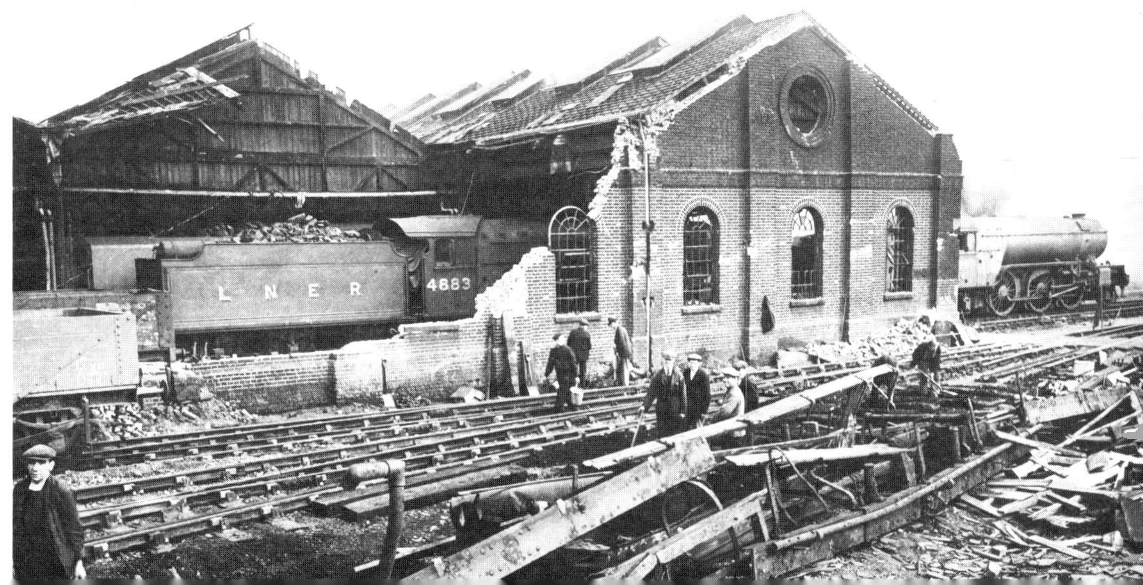

75
A rare view of 'D3' 4-4-0 No 2000 (formerly No 4075) arriving at Kings Cross (with a burnt smokebox door) on an officers' special, 1 December 1944. This was its first outing on such a working. Brass capped chimney, tender carrying LNER coat of arms and 'NE'. *C. C. B. Herbert*

76
'K4' 2-6-0 No 3445 *MacCailin Mór* was rebuilt as a two-cylinder locomotive in December 1945 and initially classified 'K1'. Here it passes New Southgate with an up goods on 23 April 1946.
E. R. Wethersett/Ian Allan Library

77
'C1' 4-4-2 No 3293 was fitted with Westinghouse continuous cab signalling equipment in March 1946 and is seen at Kings Cross shed in the September of that year.

it was later given No 2000. The purpose of this refurbishing was to provide an engine to work officers' special trains. One such occasion was on 29 November 1944 leaving Kings Cross at 11.50 for York whence a return was made two days later. The need for a special engine on these duties was infrequent and then at widely spaced locations. The home shed was Grantham.

Continuing his efforts to produce a suitable standard mixed traffic Pacific engine, Thompson modified the highly successful Gresley 'V2' 2-6-2 design so what was to have been the final four 'V2s' emerged from Darlington as Class A2/1 Pacifics. After lengthy running-in from Darlington shed the first of these, No 3696 appeared at Kings Cross taking the 13.40 Hull express on 21 November 1944. By January 1945 two of these Pacifics, Nos 3696/7 were allocated to Kings Cross shed whence they worked turn about with other Pacific classes.

Early in January 1945 No 2003 *Lord President* moved south to Top Shed in readiness for trials with other Pacifics. It was first seen taking the 15.21 to Cambridge on 5 January. Next day it went through to Leeds with the 13.15 from Kings Cross and returned the following morning on the 7.50 ex-Leeds. This train left Grantham 11min late loaded to 18 bogies and was stopped out of course at Peterborough, suffered two pw checks afterwards and arrived in London still 11min late. The trials took place later that month. 'A2/2' No 2003, 'A2/1' No 3697 and 'A4' No 2512 *Silver Fox* were all tested in turn on the 10.30 Kings Cross-Leeds and 7.50 return next day; the 9.40 Kings Cross-Grantham and 15.17 return same day and finally on the 10.53 braked goods Kings Cross to Doncaster returning next day at 9.26. Weather and operating conditions were both poor, spoiling the trials to such an extent they were repeated in May with better results. On this occasion only two trains were used; 10.30 Kings Cross-Grantham and 15.17 return express passenger and 00.25 Kings Cross-New England returning at 4.50 to East Goods. Published results showed the 'A4' as lightest on coal working passenger trains whilst No 3697 was lightest on the braked goods duties. Passenger train loads were usually 17/18 coaches weighing from 550-580ton and the goods were from 505-706ton.

By far the greatest sensation came in September 1945. The original Gresley 'A1' Pacific No 4470 *Great Northern* had been drastically rebuilt by Thompson as his proposed class 'A' standard express engine. It was exhibited at Marylebone on 27 September after which it travelled back to Doncaster via Harringay spur. After a spell working from Doncaster shed this rebuild worked through to London on 22 October arriving at 14.00 and returned north at 15.45. In the following week No 4470 was transferred to Top Shed for use on normal duties operated from there.

The sight of this ungainly looking machine aroused the wrath of every Gresley supporter. No matter what the future might hold, in their eyes Thompson had perpetrated an unforgivable outrage for which he would never receive forgiveness. Forebodings were heightened in converstation with a young Doncaster apprentice, then doing a spell of footplate riding, who declared that it was said 'The *Scotsman* is to be the next conversion'. Happily it was not. The apprentice worked his way up to the top, becoming one of the best known Locomotive Running men on British Railways.

Another Thompson rebuild, this time a conversion from Class B17 to B2 No 2871 *Manchester City* reached Kings Cross from Cambridge at 17.20 on 18 October 1945. In its lined green livery it was destined to become the 'Royal Engine' for which purpose it was renamed *Royal Sovereign* in February 1946.

The war having ended in the spring of 1945, little time was lost in repatriating the War Department 2-8-0s from France and Belgium. Several were once more soon working restored fast coal trains between Peterborough and Hornsey. At the same time all coal and returned empties were upgraded from Class C to A with smaller loads worked by 'K3' or 'V2' engines. This move meant quicker transits and enabled the elderly Gresley 2-8-0s of Class O2 and O3 to be transferred to lighter work at Grantham, Doncaster and Colwick.

On the locomotive side in 1945 matters were rather quieter. Thompson's new 'L1' 2-6-4T, No 9000 was inspected at Kings Cross on 5 June after which it took the 7.15 Kings Cross-Letchworth on 6th and 12th returning with the 12.35 from Hitchin but on 13th it had commenced trials from Stratford shed. It was transferred to Kings Cross on 30 August to undertake a number of trips to Cambridge leaving London at 12.20 and returning from Cambridge at 17.25, both of which stopped all stations north of Hatfield. After two weeks No 9000 moved over to Neasden.

A very unusual type seen in Kings Cross station with a parcels train on 7 August was 'B8' No 5448 from Colwick.

Back in 1944 the LNER had commenced building standard LMS '8F' 2-8-0s at Doncaster and Darlington of which No 8513 (Doncaster Works No 1959 of 1944) was stationed at New England shed working coal trains and returned empties up to Hornsey. In mid-year both Gresley 'P1' 2-8-2 Mikados Nos 2393/4, which since 1935 had been used on normal 80 wagon loads, were withdrawn. Their end was hastened by the decision to eliminate heavy slow moving coal trains in favour of faster and lighter hauls combined with the need for their boilers as spares for 'A3' Pacifics.

Coming restoration of suburban trains to Broad Street was foreshadowed on 16 July 1945 when an unidentified 'N2' 0-6-2T was seen at Broad Street propelling a goods brake van occupied by drivers learning the road. Resumption came on 30 July when a limited peak hour service of five trains from GN stations began. All trains were composed of standard Gresley eight-coach articulated sets hauled by 'N2s'. Thus, just over 70 years after the North London Railway commenced operating its own trains from the City terminus to GN destinations, the LNER assumed responsibility. The timetable dated 1 October 1945 gave five morning arrivals at Broad Street between 8.22 and 9.44, three from Hertford North, one from Welwyn Garden City and one from Gordon Hill which was unusual in that it ran non-stop from Palmers Green to Finsbury Park. The 7.35 ex-Hertford was unusually routed via Cole Green to Welwyn Garden City whence it called all stations to New Barnet, then Finsbury Park to reach Broad Street at 8.46 — only 10min before the 7.58 from Hertford via Enfield Chase arrived. The 7.35 commenced its journey as the 6.19 Finsbury Park-Hertford via Enfield. The evening service from Broad Street commenced with 16.10 and 16.40 all stations to Hertford; then 17.10 Welwyn Garden City which was non-stop from Finsbury Park to Hadley Wood for which 13min were allowed. This train perpetuated the prewar 17.12 to Potters Bar allowed 13min non-stop from Finsbury Park to New Barnet with LMS 0-6-0T ('Jinty') haulage. The last two departures were at 17.27 all stations to Cuffley and 17.54 all to New Barnet. Saturday morning arrivals were identical with other weekdays but departures were 12.14 Cuffley; 12.32 Hatfield; 12.44 New Barnet; 13.14 Gordon Hill and 13.28 Hertford via Enfield. All Broad Street trains called at Dalston Jct in either direction.

Because the non-electrified part of Moorgate terminus had been severely damaged by wartime bombing it was not possible to restore the through trains from GN stations until 1946. On 1 October 1945 a service of six morning trains was put on to Aldersgate; two each from Hatfield and New Barnet and one each from Hertford and Gordon Hill. Three of these formed northbound departures at 8.32 and 9.18 for Hertford and 9.33 to Hatfield. A like number of departures in the evenings went to Hertford North (3), Cuffley, Potters Bar and Welwyn Garden City (1 each). The first left at 16.47 and the last at 17.43. Saturday morning arrivals were as on Monday-Friday but there were only four northbound departures between 11.59 and 12.55, one each to Hertford, Cuffley, Gordon Hill and New Barnet. Moorgate was re-opened on 6 May 1946. There was an additional up morning train from Gordon Hill otherwise the previous Aldersgate trains were extended. Nine evening departures operated between 16.05 and 18.12, four serving Hertford, two Hatfield and one each Cuffley, Potters Bar and Welwyn Garden City. The 16.52 Moorgate-Hertford was non-stop from Finsbury Park to Palmers Green and the 18.00 to Hatfield from Finsbury Park to New Barnet. Evidence of decreasing Saturday travel was reflected by retention of four northbound departures two to Hertford and one each to Gordon Hill and New Barnet. To form departures there were four passenger carrying workings into Moorgate during the late afternoons Monday-Friday and two on Saturdays. The resumption of Moorgate trains compared unfavourably with the 1939 totals of 29 arrivals and 30 departures.

Although normally most local trains were hauled by 'N2' 0-6-2T based at Kings Cross, Hornsey and Hatfield, with some use of 'N7s' from the latter shed, Hornsey made use of 'N1' 0-6-2T about this time. Particularly on the 18.20 Finsbury Park-Hertford North.

Added interest came in the closing months of 1945 and early 1946 when numbers of 'Austerity' 2-8-0s were returning from the Continent following service with the War Department. Many travelled from south coast ports to London over Southern metals and thence via Willesden and the North London line to Canonbury where the LNER took

78

Underneath a fine gantry of GNR semaphore signals north of Finsbury Park station comes 'A3' 4-6-2 No 97 *Humorist* with the up 'Yorkshire Pullman' on its inaugural run, 4 November 1946. No 97 is in green livery with shaded numbers and 'LNER'.
K. A. C. R. Nunn/E. Neve collection

79

'B16/1' 4-6-0 No 1459 on a well-laden down goods near Hadley Wood, 28 September 1946. *H. C. Casserley*

80
'V2' 2-6-2 No 922 stands pilot at Kings Cross station, 1947, while 'A3' 4-6-2 No 56 *Centenary* awaits it return journey. *E. Neve*

81
Some heavy empty trains out of Kings Cross required double heading. The stock of the up 'Flying Scotsman' is taken past Holloway on 27 May 1947 behind 'N2' 0-6-2Ts Nos 9533 and 9505. Most of the train consists of postwar stock, but the first vehicle is a Gresley GNR carriage. *E. R. Wethersett/Ian Allan Library*

82
Two LNER quad-art sets form a down Welwyn Garden City stopping train, near New Southgate on 5 July 1947. 'N2' 0-6-2T No 9587 at the front end.
E. R. Wethersett/Ian Allan Library

over. No 77705, destined for Dundee, was derailed at Canonbury on 30 November 1945 whilst three days later a rake of four was seen en route to the north-east. The most notable sight at Canonbury was No 77486 buried in the platform ramp after demolishing a signal post. It was hauled off on 12 January 1946 by 'J52' 0-6-0T No 4257.

Another unusual sight on 12 January 1946 was SR Bulleid 0-6-0 No C35 apparently after working on to GN Section lines via Canonbury.

There was an unprecedented number of accidents between Hatfield and Kings Cross in the two years 1945-6. Sunday evening 4 February 1945 saw the most serious accident ever to happen in Kings Cross station. The 18.00 departure for Leeds headed by 'A4' No 2512 *Silver Fox* stalled in Gasworks tunnel and, without the driver realising it, ran backwards into the terminus. As soon as the signalman saw what was happening he re-set the points, which had already been altered in readiness for the 19.00 departure from No 10 platform. Unfortunately his action was seconds too late and the rear coaches of the Leeds train were derailed and collided with the front vehicles of the 19.00 'Aberdonian'. Some coaches reared on end, effectively demolishing the bridge carrying signals and cables putting platforms 6 to 17 out of action. Whilst debris was cleared all main line trains were limited to 14 vehicles and accommodated in platforms 1 to 5 which were not affected. All other trains, outer and inner suburban, terminated at or started from Finsbury Park. Two people were killed. The wrecked coaches were cleared by 13.00 next day but all points and signals relating to platforms 6-17 had to be hand operated for several days until new wiring and other equipment was installed.

Just over a year later a multiple collision occurred at Potters Bar on 19 February 1946 when the 21.32 local train from Hatfield to Kings Cross was derailed after running into buffer stops north of the station. Both fast lines were blocked and the wreckage was run into by 'V2' No 4876 hauling the 21.45 Kings Cross-Newcastle express and then by another 'V2' No 4833 on the 17.00 Bradford-Kings Cross. The latter had halted before causing much further damage but turned on to its left side. 'N2' No 2679 was on the local train. All lines were effectively blocked until 8.00 next morning. Meanwhile all trains were diverted via the Hertford loop.

This mishap was followed on 15 June when 'V2' No 3645 was derailed on the curve south of Hatfield station when hauling the relief 'Aberdonian'. Next, on 9 September a similar derailment occurred at Marshmoor, a little further south, whilst working an express from Newcastle. No serious casualties were sustained. In both instances it was found there were certain deficiencies in the track and the limited amount of lateral control on the pony trucks of the engines gave rise to derailment. Improved pony trucks having greater side control were recommended by the Inspecting Officer. Subsequently all 'V2' engines were supplied with improved pony trucks.

One of the early matters considered by E. Thompson after he took office as CME at Doncaster in 1941 was a complete renumbering scheme for locomotives. By the end of 1943 this had been outlined in draft form but wartime conditions prevented it being put into operation. Implementation of this scheme commenced on 13 January 1946 and it took just over one year to alter the numbers of the 6,263 engine concerned. Blocks were allotted to each class commencing at No 1 with the 'A4' Pacifics and progressing through the largest passenger engines and mixed traffic types until reaching 9999 given to the 'U1' Garratt (2395) and ending with 10000 the solitary 'W1'. This latter was one of only three engines which retained their old numbers, the other two being 'J3' 0-6-0s 4125/6. Not surprisingly most observers of long standing experience were not wildly enthusiastic about this massive renumbering which changed the time honoured No 4472 into 103 and 2509 to 14. Many were hard put to adjust to the changes. The situation was not helped when the Gresley Pacifics, originally allocated numbers in the series 501-613, some of which were carried, were again altered to receive numbers 1-112 and the 'V2' class changed from 700-883 to 800-983.

Although the North Eastern Railway had installed Raven Cab Signalling apparatus from 1895 onwards and retained the system in use until October 1933 by which time it had been fitted to sundry Gresley Pacifics, the LNER had not pursued the matter any further until early 1938. The disastrous collision at Castlecary on 10 December 1937, which caused 35 deaths and the Pacific No 2744 *Grand Parade* to be renewed, led to a strong recommendation from the Inspecting Officer that the LNER should look into the question of automatic train control. In May 1939 work started on equipping locomotives and track with the Hudd system of electro-magnetic control for trials on the Edinburgh-Glasgow main line. Unfortunately war conditions put a stop to all experiments of this nature and the system was dismantled. Sensing a possible market for a viable system of ATC after the war ended, the Westinghouse Co designed their Coded Continuous Cab Signalling apparatus. Permission was obtained from the LNER to equip the down main line between Greenwood Box (Hadley Wood) and Potters Bar with the necessary relays in conjunction with a modified form of track circuit. One locomotive only was equipped with a turbo-generator, receiver and four aspect miniature signal in the cab. This latter repeated the aspects of each colour light signal over the critical length of track and was reinforced by a bell warning when a more restrictive signal indication was given. The selected engine was 'C1' Atlantic No 3293 (later 2821) which was placed in the Milk Dock at Kings Cross station on 19 May 1946 for inspection purposes. No official reports on the trials of this system have been seen. It was three years before more trials with ATC were undertaken.

In May 1946 through engine workings between London and Leeds were restored using Kings Cross Pacifics. Five 'A3' were transferred to Top shed from Doncaster, Grantham and New England. These were followed in October by six more bringing the total of London Pacifics up to 34.

By the end of the war most Ivatt Atlantics were 40 years old or more. Those working in the London district had become very run-down and many were laid up out of service leaving a power shortage for the Hitchin and Cambridge line passenger trains. As a result 'K3', 'V2' and even two Hitchin 'N2' 0-6-2Ts were used on stopping trains. Use of 'J39' 0-6-0s on passenger trains had been commonplace in certain locations prewar but never in the GN London area. So it was notable on 1 July 1946 when No 2951 arrived at Kings Cross from Cambridge at 17.13. Two days later the same train had 'D9' 4-4-0 No 6040 another rare sight. The 17.50 arrival from Hitchin brought Ivatt 'D3' No 4309 on 1 July. This engine, then 48 years old was normally confined to working engineers trains from Hitchin yard. Another 'J39' took the 17.34 Baldock from Kings Cross on 15 August but more remarkable was the sight of 'Austerity' 2-8-0 No 70826 hauling an outer suburban train into the terminus on 21 August. Even more unusual was use of ex-GE 'J19/2' 0-6-0 No 4654 on the 17.10 Kings Cross-Royston on 3 September. Another GE type seen in the terminus on 20 September was 'J20' No 8279. However striking changes were in the offing. Mass withdrawal of Atlantics caused amendments to the planned allocation of new Thompson 'B1' 4-6-0s so that Hitchin began to receive some of that class in November to take over their passenger train duties.

The transfer of Neasden depot on the GC Section to the Kings Cross District meant certain repairs were undertaken at the parent shed. This resulted in unfamiliar classes appearing on the GN lines. The first recorded was 'L3' 2-6-4T No 5342 making its way back to Neasden via Harringay spur on 19 August. Another of the class, No 9055, spent some 20 days working ecs trains between Kings Cross and Hornsey in November.

Thompson's first standard 6ft 2in Pacific Classed A2 (later A2/3) was turned out of Doncaster shops in May 1946 and travelled south to Marylebone for a ceremony on 31 May when it received the name *Edward Thompson*. Not until 17 July did this new engine appear at Kings Cross on the 16.34 arrival from Hull and the next morning took the 6.00 to Cambridge. Prior to this it had been working slow trains between Doncaster, Grantham and York together with the second member of the class No 511 *Airborne* pending modification of the steam pipes. Although a second 'A2', No 513 *Dante* was allocated to Kings Cross in July, it did not arrive until 19 September. Eventually four of the class were allocated to Kings Cross, Nos 500/13/4/23 and the fifth Southern Area engine No 520 was at Doncaster. The remainder of the class were distributed between the NE Area (9) and Scottish (1).

A special high-speed trial train was run from Kings Cross to Edinburgh and back on 21 and 22 May 1946 solely to ascertain track conditions at speeds higher than those generally in force at the time. From observed data a decision was reached as to the possible relaxation of speed limits imposed during the war years. Choice of locomotives fell upon 'A4' No 2512 *Silver Fox* handled by G. Kitchener of Top Shed, one of the few drivers still in service with experience of prewar high-speed working. The load was six bogies of 207 tons gross weight. Stops were made at Grantham (105.5 miles allowed 98min), York (82.7 miles 77min), Newcastle (80.1 miles 77min) and finally

124min were allowed for the 124.4 miles on to Edinburgh. Slight adjustments were made for the return journey. Drivers were changed at York, where J. Leonard took over and at Newcastle. In the event scheduled running times for the complete journey were cut from 378½min in each direction to 368 northbound and 358¾min southbound. On the return journey a maximum of 102mile/h was attained between Little Bytham and Essendine. Altogether a satisfactory experience so soon after the end of the war confirming beyond any doubt that the 'A4s' could still deliver the goods when required subject to improved track conditions.

Re-instatement of the 'Yorkshire Pullman' came on Monday 4 November 1946. Starting from Harrogate at 10.20 and leaving Leeds at 11.03, stops were made at Wakefield (Westgate) and Doncaster, where a portion from Hull was attached. Leaving Doncaster at 11.58 the non-stop run to Kings Cross was allowed 172min for the 156 miles, 16min more than prewar. After arrival at 14.50 the return was an hour later reaching Doncaster at 18.44 and Harrogate 20.20. The selected engines were both 'A3s', No 97 *Humorist* southbound and No 107 *Royal Lancer* northbound. Both were in perfect external condition with named headboards affixed to the smokebox fronts. Arrival at Kings Cross was a minute early but it became clear when departure time arrived that Kings Cross had completely lost itsr flair for the big occasion, so admirably done in the past. The signal remained red causing the Station Master to look decidedly worried. It was not until 15.56 that the signal cleared. Further delays occurred resulting in a 15min late arrival at Leeds. Copley Hill men were responsible for all working of this train. Except on 14 November when 'A4' No 10 worked the up train the two 'A3s' maintained their workings until 18 November when No 89 *Felstead* replaced No 107. In turn No 89 gave way to 'A2' No 500 on 28 December and No 513 on 17 January. No 97 however made a very creditable record by running 58 consecutive trips down to 11 January. In addition on the days when arriving in London at 14.50 that engine also took the 19.30 'Aberdonian' to Grantham arriving back at 2.30 on the Newcastle Mail. This second duty was undertaken on 23 out of a possible 28 trips.

For the older GN line observers the daily scene was rapidly changing insofar as locomotives were concerned. None was old enough to remember times before Ivatt Atlantics were commonplace but by early 1947 those much loved engines were seen rarely and then only on menial duties. One such duty worked fairly regularly by No 2817 of Top Shed took the morning stock train down to Peterborough leaving London soon after 10.00 and returned on the stopping passenger train due into Kings Cross at 21.58 which enjoyed a non-stop run between Hitchin and Finsbury Park thus affording a nostalgic opportunity for some evening excursions by interested recorders.

By January 1947 Hitchin shed had received their full complement of 14 'B1' 4-6-0s (Nos 1089-99, 1105-7) but the Kings Cross quota of nine was not completed until July (Nos 1029 *Chamois*, 1112/3/4/21/9, 1200/3 to which Nos 1251/66 were subsequently added). Peterborough (New England) shed received Nos 1070/3/5, 1143/4, 1206/9/10. At all three sheds the 'B1' engines replaced Atlantics on all but main express duties. Those at both Kings Cross and New England were pressed into service at busy times on braked goods and relief express trains as on 23 August when No 1113 took the 19.30 Aberdeen express from Kings Cross and later two Peterborough 'B1s' were seen on the 22.55 Leeds (No 1136) and 23.15 Newcastle trains (No 1209).

There were occasional visits by strange locomotives like on 26 July when a GC Atlantic No 2903 came up from Lincoln with a nine coach relief to the morning Cleethorpes express. It remained in London until the following Tuesday before returning home on a similar train. A more unusual type seen taking a down empties from Ferme Park northwards on 16 October was 'Q6' 0-8-0 No 3397.

Longer through locomotive diagrams began to return in the summer of 1947 when the 10.00 'Flying Scotsman' engine went through to York, returning from there at 21.58 (19.30 ex-Newcastle) and the 19.40 Parcels from Kings Cross, which ran non-stop to Doncaster, was frequently 'B1' worked. This latter duty had a similar back working next day. Crews changed at Peterborough on the 10.00 diagram and Doncaster on the 19.40. A welcome return of Tyneside Pacifics came with the winter 1947 timetable when two weekday workings brought them up from Grantham into London at 13.35 and 15.30 with returns at 17.30 and 19.00 ('Aberdonian'). After servicing these Pacifics went forward to Newcastle later the same night. York engines were diagrammed to arrive in London at 3.00 and 7.15 returning at 10.00 and 13.00 on which duties 'A2/3' Nos 522 *Straight Deal* and 524 *Herringbone* were regularly employed, with 'V2s' used at times. The London engine diagrams to York were changed, leaving at 1.00 and 4.25 they were due back at 13.25 and 18.55 respectively.

In mid-1947 the LNER announced plan to construct 25 diesel-electric locomotives of 1,600hp to haul Anglo-Scottish expresses. It was envisaged these units would work in pairs about 30 trains daily over the ECML. Maximum speeds of 100mile/h were planned and it was estimated that 32 Pacifics would be released for other duties. This latter view seemed somewhat vague bearing in mind there were then no less than 84 steam Pacifics on order. However, the plan was not destined to bear fruit and it was 10 years before the first diesel locomotives began to appear on the ECML.

With the end of 1947 in sight, plans to Nationalise all railways in Britain were well advanced to take effect on 1 January 1948. Speculation amongst the platform-end observers as to possible effects varied according to political beliefs. Many railwaymen confidently predicted a most rosy future under the new regime. Both sides were uncertain of the true outcome, going forward into a new era for the second time within a quarter-century.

The 'Yorkshire Pullman' resumed on 6 October 1947, following withdrawal during the coal crisis. Once again 'A3' Pacifics were used; No 60104 *Solario* reached Kings Cross right time with the southbound run but No 60105 *Victor Wild* was delayed 2-3min starting due to an empty train being sent out ahead. Then, whilst, ascending the gradient in Gasworks tunnel the engine slipped to a standstill. The guard left his train to walk back towards Kings Cross to protect it but on turning round saw the train had gone. He walked rapidly to the signalbox whence a message was despatched to Finsbury Park for the train to be stopped. Meantime both 16.00 and 16.10 expresses had been despatched via the slow line and the guard had to wait for the 16.15 semi-fast to take him out and rejoin his charge which finally left Finsbury Park around 16.25.

1948-1955

British Railways inherited from the LNER in January 1948 roughly the same number of passenger trains, express and slow, as did the LNER in January 1923. The greatest contrast was provided by goods and mineral trains which had been vastly accelerated by 1948 when about a dozen weekday services from New England to Ferme Park ran at class A speeds taking around four hours for the 73-mile journey as compared with double the number in 1923 taking 8 hours or more at the slower class C speed. The passenger trains were handled by Gresley and Thompson Pacific classes and by Gresley 'V2s' whilst the goods and mineral hauls were mainly in the hands of 'Austerity' 2-8-0s, purchased from the Ministry of Supply by the LNER who classified them '07'.

Apart from the complete re-numbering described in the previous chapter much interest was aroused by changes in liveries. Back in August 1946 the LNER started to restore lined green livery for passenger engines. Early examples were in the north-east and did not appear in London. The first Top Shed Pacific repainted was No 89 *Felstead* in March 1947. The special Garter blue livery was restored to 'A4' Pacifics from June 1946 when the famous *Silver Link* came out of shops so painted and carrying the new number 14. Lettering and numerals were cut-out metal Gill Sans style.

Before the wartime unlined black livery had disappeared completely, British Railways commenced experiments with a variety of liveries. During April-June 1948 seven 'A3s' all in the NE Region were given a dark blue colour, lined out in cream and red. Of these No 60091 *Captain Cuttle*, which had to be transferred from Carlisle to Gateshead in order to show off the new livery to greater advantage, did

visit London occasionally. A similar dark blue (almost purple) shade appeared on certain 'A4s' in mid-1948 when two Kings Cross engines, Nos 60028/9 were so treated. At the same time they carried the letters 'British Railways' on the tender. Meanwhile the 'A3s' continued to receive lined green livery, apart from the blue painted examples mentioned above, until May 1949 when a darker blue shade with black and white lining became standard for all 6ft 8in Pacifics

New locomotive classes continued to appear in London during 1948 beginning on 11 March when No E530 *Sayajirao*, the first 'A2' Pacific incorporating Peppercorn amendments to the Thompson design of 1946-7, arrived at Kings Cross shed to join the Thompson variety Nos 500/13/4/23. These 'A2' engines did not remain long at Top Shed. In May 1948 No 523 moved to Leeds and in December all except No 500 went to New England where No 523 joined them. On 18 August the first Peppercorn 'A1' No 60114 made its maiden trip to London arriving at 14.40 on the West Riding express. Two days later it took the 17.50 Hull down to Doncaster. At a ceremony held in Platform 12 in the Local station at Kings Cross No 60114 was named *W. P. Allen* the Trade Union member of the Railway Executive who had been a cleaner on the GNR and progressed to engine driver. From 2 November the new Pacific regularly worked the 13.30 to Doncaster, returning into Kings Cross at 21.50. This was a newly introduced engine and men diagram and the first regular out and home working by London men to Doncaster with same engine for many years.

Beyond any doubt the greatest events of postwar locomotive running were the Interchange Trials between engines of the four groups running express trains on each of the four new BR regions. So far as Kings Cross was concerned events began

83
'Royal Scot' 4-6-0 No 46162 *Queen's Westminster Rifleman* at Finsbury Park with a Kings Cross-Leeds express during the Interchange Trials of 1948. *Derrick A. Dant*

on Monday 19 April 1948 when LMS 'Royal Scot' No 46162 took out the 13.10 to Leeds, returning next day at 7.50 due Kings Cross 12.15. These preliminary runs were repeated on the next two days whilst 'A4' No 60034 was undergoing dynamometer car tests on the same trains going down on Tuesday and Thursday and back on Wednesday and Friday. During the following week LMS Pacific No 46236 commenced preliminary runs whilst No 46162 did test runs. No preliminary runs were made on 3 May but No 46236 went on trial on 4 May.

GWR 'King' No 6018 commenced preliminary runs on 10 May and test runs a week later when SR 'Merchant Navy' No 35019 made a preliminary run on 17 and 18 May but was replaced by No 35017 on 20th, due to a blow hole in a thermic syphon.

Intense interest was aroused by the work of these 'foreign' engines on the ECML by both observers and railwaymen alike. Photographers were out in force securing shots in profusion. Timekeeping on arrivals in London was remarkably good, the latest being 4min late. Naturally all the visiting enginemen had the services of LNER conductor drivers. For the 7.50 ex-Leeds Grantham supplied the conductor into Kings Cross. On the occasion of the 'Royal Scot's' first trial up run there was a hiatus at Peterborough. The train was running slightly late and the Camden driver ignored the conductor's advice to reduce speed to 20mile/h for the reverse curves through the station. Just how fast the train was travelling is not known but according to the conductor only a miracle prevented derailment. The reason for this happening was due to the Camden driver's obsession that come what may he was going to be on time into London. The resulting ill-feeling between drivers caused the Grantham man to go straight to Liverpool Street after arrival in London to ask the Locomotive Running Superindent, to replace him on the next assignment. By pure chance the author met this driver on his return to Kings Cross and was told the fúll story some three hours after the event. Regrettably no published record of that run has been seen but on his next trip the LMS driver was recorded as passing Peterborough at 23mile/h and the substitute Grantham conductor told me he had no trouble that day.

In order to provide three Kylchap 'A4s' for the trials Nos 22, 60033/4 were transferred to Kings Cross from Grantham in exchange for Nos 21/5/6 with single chimneys. In the days preceding *Mallard's* visit to the Western Region for trials there had been anxiety over the state of the middle big end but the Mechanical Foreman at Top shed was advised to re-metal it but he resisted. On the first preliminary trip from Paddington to Plymouth the big-end gave out near Savernake and No 22 was replaced by No 60033 *Seagull* for the remaining tests. Top shed's driver Burgess put up an excellent performance with this engine and on the occasion of his final test run into Paddington a group of East Coast supporters made it their business to witness the arrival. To their lasting satisfaction a GWR inspector was heard to remark 'We have nothing to touch this engine'. Praise indeed from the opposition.

Tests on the Ferme Park (Hornsey) to Peterborough stretch with heavy goods engines were also conducted, but little of these was seen by the general public. Engines tested were 'Austerity' 2-10-0 No 73776 and 2-8-0 No 63169; ER 'O1' 2-8-0 No 63773; LMR '8F' No 48189 and WR 2-8-0 No 3803.

After this excitement more mundane events paled somewhat. There was a resumption of engine cleaning at Kings Cross in February 1948 with immensely beneficial results. One notable feature was that the two regular crews on 'N2' No 69571 maintained their engine in a very fine condition.

A fresh type used on the Finsbury Park-Alexandra Palace pull and push trains was 'C12' Ivatt 4-4-2T No 67374 suitably equipped with the required gear. Thus Ivatt's first 'Met Tank' design returned to its original haunts after an absence of 27 years.

For a three week period early in 1948 Hatfield sent their 'N2' 0-6-2T No 69537 down into Moorgate chimney first — a hitherto unknown event and it was also noticed the same shed used non-condensing 'N2s' with the large chimneys on Moorgate trains. This became possible due to destruction of Smithfield Meat Market during the war which removed the restricting pipes over the line.

A feature of the 1948 summer timetable introduced on 31 May was the restoration of the 'Flying Scotsman's' 392¾-mile non-stop run between Kings Cross and Edinburgh each way. For this 7hr 50min were allowed compared with a level 7hr in 1939. In a downpour of rain together with much official activity and the 'right away' given by

84
'C12' 4-4-2T No 7374 propelling an Alexandra Palace-Finsbury Park push-pull train. *P. Ransome-Wallis*

85
'N1' 0-6-2T No 9460 at the entrance to Gasworks tunnel, Kings Cross, 1948. *E. Neve*

86
Un-named 'A1' 4-6-2 No 60115 approaches Finsbury Park and is checked by signals with the up 'Tees-Tyne Pullman' on its inaugural run, 27 September 1948. *K. A. C. R. Nunn/E. Neve collection*

the Lord Mayor of London, the first postwar non-stop pulled out behind 'A4' No 60034 *Lord Faringdon* driven by E. Moore. Ill fortune dogged Haymarket's No 60009 on the southbound run. It was stopped north of Newcastle by an aircraft accident and again at Grantham due to a damaged water scoop, finally passing Wood Green some 25min late.

Only one through engine working from Tyneside to Kings Cross featured in the new timetable. Leaving Newcastle at 12.5 the train was publicly booked non-stop from York to Kings Cross, arrive, 17.35 but in fact called at Peterborough to change crews. Return was on the 22.15 'Night Scotsman'. Initially it was worked by a spotless Heaton 'A3' No E72 *Sunstar*.

Once more Leeds, Copley Hill, shed acquired a stud of Pacifics to cover through diagrams to London. 'A3s' Nos 46/56/62 moved from Kings Cross together with 'A2/3' No 523 and 'A2' No 533 moved from New England to Leeds. Three weekday diagrams were rostered, leaving Leeds at 7.50, 9.50 and 11.00. Reaching Kings Cross at 12.15, 13.55 and 14.50 they returned at 15.50, 16.00 and 18.05.

An interesting Peterborough diagram at this time brought a Pacific or 'V2' into London at 13.25 on the 8.52 ex-Sunderland, returning on the 15.30 Glasgow braked goods. A limited number of braked goods had been restored in the winter of 1947-8, seven at No 1 speed and eight at No 2 speed. There were also a number running at a new No 3 speed without vacuum brake. To test suitability on this work on LMR Class 4F 2-6-0 No 43018 appeared at Kings Cross on 14 July, taking a No 1 goods to New England whence it returned at 23.35 on a No 3 unbraked train.

A second prewar Pullman service was restored on 5 July when the 'Queen of Scots' left Kings Cross at 11.30 headed by 'A3' No 60107 *Royal Lancer* with 10 cars, eight of which went to Glasgow and two were detached at Leeds to return on the southbound train, headed by another 'A3' No 60109 *Hermit*. Both were London engines with balancing duties on the 8.45 Kings Cross-Leeds to return thence at 16.30 on the Pullman whilst the 'down' Pullman engine returned from Leeds on a braked goods at 20.00. It was intended that Leeds crews should operate the Pullmans through to London on a lodging basis, but they declined. For a while both trains stopped at Grantham to change crews which depot covered the whole duties.

To provide better facilities between Tyneside and Tees-side to London an entirely new Pullman train was put on from 27 September 1948. Although earlier reports had suggested this would be a restoration of the famed 'Silver Jubilee', it materialised as an all-Pullman train named 'Tees-Tyne Pullman'. Starting from Newcastle one hour earlier than the 'Jubilee' at 9.00 it called at Darlington and then to Grantham to change enginemen before reaching Kings Cross at 14.16. Return was at 17.30, like the prewar streamliner and, with the same stops as southbound, reached Newcastle at 22.50. Heaton engines were diagrammed through to London, returning the same evening on the down train. At first 'A1' No 60115 was borrowed from Gateshead pending arrival of Heaton's first 'A1' No 60116. During the early weeks of operation Heaton 'A3s' Nos 69, 60072/85 also appeared. The uneconomic working method lasted only until the summer timetable of 1949 when Kings Cross engines and men took over the duties, going through to Newcastle, lodging and returning next day. Balancing turns operated on Saturday and Sunday.

The resumption of lodging duties at Top Shed commenced in May 1948 when the Edinburgh non-stop resumed. Now only Kings Cross and Haymarket crews were involved using 'A4' engines. To provide for this a new No 1 Link was formed at Kings Cross comprising eight sets recruited from the existing 20 set Main Line Passenger Link. In addition to the two crews needed each day for the non-stop duties, the new link had three turns to Grantham, two to Peterborough and one week on pilot turn. The Main Line Passenger Link was made up of 16 crews who had turns to Doncaster (1), Grantham (9), Peterborough (4) and two pilot weeks.

In 1946 the 10.00 'Flying Scotsman' was worked throughout to Newcastle by Grantham engines and men, changing at Grantham and then running non-stop to Newcastle. For this latter stage Grantham maintained certain 'A4s' in pristine condition and it soon became a tradition that however late the train left Grantham because of delays further south, it was on time at Newcastle. Grantham men had to leave their engine at Newcastle for reconditioning and return home on the 'Afternoon Scotsman' with a Gateshead 'A4' whilst their own returned during the night. However in June 1947 the 10.00 resumed its wartime stop at

Peterborough, thence non-stop to York and the Grantham men took the preceding 9.50 Glasgow express to Newcastle instead.

Because timekeeping on the down 'Flying Scotsman' was often very poor the Peterborough stop was once more omitted in favour of one at Grantham in September 1948. Now Grantham shed was responsible for working the famous train throughout from London to Newcastle. Two engines were set aside for the diagram. The first left Grantham at 4.37 to London reached at 7.05 before taking the 10.00 down to Grantham where it was removed in favour of the second engine for the run to Newcastle. The engine working to London on MWF went to Newcastle on T/Th/S and vice versa. At first 'A3' No 60039 *Sandwich* and 'A4' No 60030 *Golden Fleece* were regularly used. Grantham enginemen were jubilant at recovering this prestige turn and no effort was spared to run the 'Scotsman' to time. For the first time since 1939 there was one Grantham-London-York-Grantham duty commencing from Grantham at 13.27 to London (15.30), then 19.00 'Aberdonian' to York before returning during the night to Grantham. For some time 'A4' No 60021 *Wild Swan* did this turn.

A stranger seen in Kings Cross at 16.47 on 11 October 1948 was streamlined 'B17' No 61659 *East Anglian*, making its second appearance on the GN line after transfer from Norwich to Cambridge for a few weeks. The first appearance had been back in 1937 hauling the new 'East Anglian' train set.

There was a resumption of through Gateshead engine workings to London in November 1948 when their 'A4s' Nos 60018/9/23 began to appear on the 'Night Scotsman' arriving at 6.40 and returning home on the 13.15 express. York still provided power for the 2.55 arrival and 10.05 departure on which 'A2' No 60532 *Blue Peter* was a regular performer.

When, in its early days, the Thompson 'B1' No 1005 *Bongo* was used by Cambridge for Kings Cross trains, local observers decided this unusual name would serve as a nickname for the class. They began referring to them as 'Bongos' and this soon spread to enginemen. Reference in certain enthusiast journals to this name roused the ire of the LNER PRO who demanded it be dropped. Of course the editors of these publications had no choice but to comply in order to protect their interests. Justice seemed to be done in the winter of 1948 when a painted sign appeared on the wall behind No 14 platform at Kings Cross reading 'Stop Bongo'. This was for the benefit of drivers working the class on suburban trains needing to use the water column.

Carrying the revised name 'Cambridge Buffet Express' a service of four express trains was put on from 6 December 1948 affording a much needed improvement in the weekday timetable. Stops were made at Welwyn Garden City, Hitchin and Letchworth by all trains, with some stopping also at Baldock or Royston. The best overall schedule was 82min — 10 min more than prewar. Both 'B1' and 'B17' engines were used by Cambridge with the 'B2' No 61671 *Royal Sovereign* sometimes working the 16.47 into Kings Cross and 20.30 return. Eight coaches were rostered for the four Cambridge worked trains but the 9.35 and 14.25 from London, worked by Hitchin, had only six coaches.

During December 1948 and January 1949 all the Eastern Region 6ft 2in Pacifics of Thompson and Peppercorn design, except No 60500 which remained at Kings Cross, were transferred to New England from where the Gresley 'A3s' Nos 60052/111 moved to Doncaster and eventually eight 'A3s' were released from GN sheds to the GC section.

Six Thompson 'L1' 2-6-4T Nos 67740/1/3-6 were transferred to Hitchin late in 1948 for use on those outer-suburban duties involving tender first working previously. Nevertheless Hitchin drivers disliked bunker-first running on the main line and religiously turned their engines at Kings Cross. For a period of some three weeks prior to Easter the turntable in Kings Cross station was under repair so all tender engines had to go up to Top Shed to turn. The Hitchin men perforce had to take their 'L1s' back home without turning and occasionally they had one on the 9.35 'Cambridge Buffet Express' running bunker-first! Since some Hitchin diagrams allowed up to 3h 30min lay-over in London attention was drawn to the need for improved utilisation.

Normal power tests with 'A2' No 60539 *Bronzino*, the only double chimney member of that class, were undertaken on the 13.00 Kings Cross-Leeds on 26/28 April, returning from Leeds at 9.50 the following day. 'A1' No 60114 was similarly tested commencing 3 May. In every case loads were 500ton northbound and 481ton return.

87
The down non-stop 'Flying Scotsman' ascends Holloway Bank behind 'A4' 4-6-2 No 60029 *Woodcock* on 25 June 1948. *K. A. C. R. Nunn/E. Neve collection*

88 The Locomotive Exchange of 1948
'Merchant Navy' 4-6-2 No 35019 *French Line CGT* south of Potters Bar on 17 May 1948 with the 13.10 Kings Cross-Leeds. *Derrick A. Dant*

89
'J52' 0-6-0ST No 68825 at Hornsey shed, 1949. *Frank F. Moss*

90
A cross-London goods at Kensal Green Junction heading for Ferme Park behind 'J50' 0-6-0T No 68961. *BR*

91
'B17' 4-6-0 No 61627 *Aske Hall* on an up Cambridge Buffet express at Red Hall, south of Hatfield in 1949.
F. R. Hebron/Rail Archive Stephenson

92
'B1' 4-6-0 No 1200 on a down Cambridge train between Welwyn South and North Tunnels in 1947.
F. R. Hebron/Rail Archive Stephenson

Between 17 and 20 May high power tests were made using the 10.00 to Grantham and back with the 'Flying Scotsman' same day. Loads were 610 and 615ton respectively. An interesting feature was that trains were banked out of Kings Cross whereas Gresley Pacifics had taken similar or greater loads unbanked for several years.

For the summer of 1949 it was decided to alter the times of the non-stop London-Edinburgh trains, leaving the 'Flying Scotsman' to make the usual intermediate calls at Grantham and Newcastle. Therefore the non-stop was named the 'Capitals Limited'. It left Kings Cross at 9.30 and Edinburgh at 9.45 on an 8hr schedule — 1 hour longer than prewar. Engines used on the first day were 'A4' Nos 60010 and 60027. After No 60010 had been attached to the down train and the 'Flying Scotsman' roofboards changed to 'Capitals Limited' on the stock, the empty coaches off the up 'Aberdonian' were sent out ahead and stalled on the bank up to Holloway. A naming ceremony of the new train was performed by Miss Ann Crawford, actress, and the start delayed for 12min owing to the stalled stock train ahead.

By this time difficulties over long-distance workings had begun to sort themselves out. Copley Hill men brought up the 'Yorkshire Pullman' into Kings Cross and returned home with a different engine at 15.45. Kings Cross engines and men took the 17.30 Pullman down to Leeds, lodged and returned home next day on the 9.50 from Leeds. There were five weekday Kings Cross diagrams to York, two from York to London and still the one from Gateshead arriving at 6.40. In July this latter worked back at 10.10 instead of 15.30. New Peppercorn 'A1' Pacifics were entering service rapidly, divided between the principal main line depots when first allocated to: Kings Cross Nos 60120/3/30/1/9; Grantham Nos 60117/33/48/9; Doncaster Nos 60123/5/44/6; Copley Hill Nos 60118/9/28/34/6. Later in 1949 three more with roller bearings, numbered 60156/7/8 were also sent to Kings Cross shed.

To replace ageing ex-GC 2-4-2T on the Alexandria Palace pull and push trains another Ivatt 4-4-2T, No 67356 arrived to join No 67374. Then there were three C12 in London as another, No 67376 had been put into use in 1946 as a stationary boiler in Hornsey carriage sidings where it remained until 1951 before returning to New England for normal use.

In the summer months of 1949 there was a 17.25 Royston-Welwyn Garden City passenger train worked by Cambridge engines, which returned empty to Hitchin for the engine to turn in readiness to take the 20.46 slow to Cambridge. On six successive occasions it had 'B17' 61654 (Cambridge), 'J15' No E5391 (Cambridge); 'J39' No 4820 (Ipswich); 'D16/3' No 62516 (Cambridge); 'B1' No 61300 (Cambridge) and 'L1' No 67712 (Stratford). On other Cambridge workings numerous 'Claud Hamilton' 4-4-0s were noted, including Nos 62571/4 of Cambridge and No 62615 of Bury-St-Edmunds on 'Buffet Expresses' to Kings Cross. On 20 September surprise was caused when 'C12' No 67354 appeared on the 17.25 from Royston.

During October new 'A1s' Nos 60156/7 were put on the 'Tees-Tyne' Pullman diagram by Kings Cross shed. By then this depot housed no fewer than 38 Pacifics — an unprecedented total far beyond the capacity of the shed to maintain them adequately.

Some much-needed improvements were made in the suburban timetable commencing 26 September 1949 including the 17.34 Moorgate-Welwyn Garden City booked non-stop from Farringdon to Finsbury Park in 11min. The advent of the first postwar suburban train not calling at Kings Cross aroused considerable interest, as did the sight of three down trains leaving Finsbury Park in the space of 2min between 17.50-52. However, the new arrangement got off to a bad start when the Moorgate train stopped at Kings Cross to change crews (as per diagram), and the engine, 'N2' No 69540 lost time due to bad steaming thereafter. No 69497 was provided next day and regularly after, making a good job of the duty. The diagram was amended to eliminate crew change at Kings Cross.

Refurbished vehicles from the prewar 'West Riding Limited', with underframe skirtings removed and repainted in standard BR livery appeared in the 'West Riding' express.

Hitchin turntable was damaged by a locomotive falling into the pit in August 1949 causing havoc to the outer suburban and Cambridge diagrams. Many 'B1s' were sent light from Hitchin to Cambridge for turning whilst 'L1' 2-6-4T had to work bunker first into London. A 'J39' 0-6-0 No 4939 took the 17.39 Kings Cross to Baldock on 26 September.

A noteworthy event in late 1949 was the arrival

from Scotland of all six 'A2/2' Pacifics — the rebuilds from Gresley 'P2' 2-8-2. Nos 60504/5/6 were transferred to New England in exchange for 'A2/1' No 60507 and 'A2' Nos 60530/6. At the same time York received Nos 60501/2/3. All six were soon seen in London mainly working braked goods and slower passenger or parcels trains.

A time honoured custom dating back to Stirling days at least, was ended late in 1949 when a main line pilot engine ceased to be provided at Kings Cross station. In early LNER days the pilot was a large Atlantic accompanied at certain times by a 4-4-0. Just prior to the war the pilot was usually an 'A1' or 'A3' Pacific and afterwards more often a 'V2' 2-6-2.

Mishaps in the district during January 1950 were frequent. On 16 January 'A1' No 60127 derailed in Kings Cross yard when backing on to the 17.35 Newcastle express trapping the 17.30 'Yorkshire Pullman' which eventually left behind 'A3' No 60089 at 19.53 after further delay due to a points failure. More unusual was the derailment of 'K3' No 61811 at Holloway South on 2 January. This engine had been released from an up goods in East Goods yard to proceed into Top Shed, but was stopped by signal at Holloway South Up box. Soon a signal turned green and the driver moved off only to find his engine turned over on its left side at the catch points below the fly-over. The signal had not been for him but for a South London goods on the slow line. This particular driver had shortly before been learning the road from Hitchin to London and boasting to London men in the Top Shed mess room that there was 'nothing to it'. To the Cockneys this incident proved highly amusing. On Sunday 8 January No 61811 was re-railed by both Kings Cross and New England cranes.

Heaton Pacifics continued their daily workings into London, arriving at 13.35 and going back at 17.35. Mostly three beautifully groomed 'A3s' were used, Nos 60080 *Dick Turpin*, 60082 *Neil Gow* and 60091 *Captain Cuttle*.

Much prominence was given in enthusiast journals to the high number of engine failures, often creating an entirely false impression of the causes. Examples of such causes were as on 21 February when 'A4' No 60010 failed on the northbound 'Yorkshire Pullman' because the whistle-pipe fractured. Next day 'V2' No 60928 working the return leg from Leeds from running well when the brick arch collapsed.

Commencing 13 March Immingham 'B1' 4-6-0s began working through to London on the morning express from Cleethorpes reaching Kings Cross at 13.20 and going home with the 16.00. Hitherto this train had changed engines at Peterborough and had until late 1949 been frequently in the hands of 'A2' Pacifics. Advent of 'B1s' caused this previously good timekeeper to run late even though allowed 91min for the $76\frac{1}{4}$ miles from Peterborough with a light load of 8/9 bogies. The cause appeared to be bad steaming.

Agreement was reached for the newly built 'A1' Pacifics to be named. The first example seen was No 60133 *Pommern* of Grantham on 15 April.

On Maundy Thursday 6 April 1950 an experiment was carried out to relieve congestion at Kings Cross caused by additional trains. Four up and five down trains were diverted to Broad Street all were Cambridge, Baldock, Peterborough or Grantham services. Two 'Cambridge Buffet Expresses', were hauled by 'B17' engines despite that class not being officially authorised for Broad Street working. No engine was sent to Broad Street to take the 16.10 Grantham train which eventually left behind 'N2' No 69524 which had taken the empty stock in. At Finsbury Park the 'N2' was replaced by 'B1' No 1139.

A familiar landmark disappeared on Sunday 21 May 1950 when the large signal gantry carrying 14 GNR somersault arms, just north of Finsbury Park, was replaced by colour lights with direction indicators.

To celebrate the Centenary of opening the GNR to London a special train organised by 'Railway Pictorial' was taken from Kings Cross to York by 'A1/1' *Great Northern* carrying a large portrait of Edmund Denison 'Father of the Great Northern Railway' and its Chairman from 1847-64. Building of the 49 Peppercorn 'A1' Pacifics had been completed in December 1949. In July 1950 allocation of the Eastern Region Pacific stock was:

Class	*A1*	*A2*	*A3*	*A4*	*Total*
Kings Cross (34A)	12		10	17	39
New England (35A)	1	10			11
Grantham (35B)			2	2	4
Doncaster (36A)			6		6
Copley Hill (37B)	10		5		15

This reflects the diagramming of through engine workings from sheds at the main route terminals,

93
Un-named 'A1' 4-6-2 No 60128 approaches Hatfield with the down 'West Riding', 13 August 1948. The leading coaches are former 'Coronation' stock.
C. W. Foster

94
The first postwar non-stop 'Flying Scotsman' at Kings Cross awaits departure behind 'A4' 4-6-2 No 60034 *Lord Faringdon*. *E. Neve*

95
'B16' 4-6-0s were frequent visitors to the south of the GN main line in postwar days. No 61460 passes Little Bytham with an up goods. *P. H. Wells*

96
Ivatt Atlantic swansong. No 2881 restarts a down stopping train from Potters Bar during 1948. Note the Gresley steel-panelled twin at the front. *Derrick A. Dant*

97
A regular double-headed turn, the 17.52 from Kings Cross, seen with 'B1' 4-6-0 No 61075 and 'B2' 4-6-0 No 61671 *Royal Sovereign* at New Southgate, 13 August 1952. *E. R. Wethersett/Ian Allan Library*

98
Wood Green, 20 July 1952. 'N2' 0-6-2T No 69586 leaves with the 9.24 Kings Cross-Hertford North. *A. R. Carpenter*

London, Leeds and Newcastle and the relegation of Grantham to a re-manning point apart from a few less important duties by their small allocation. In the timetable of 28 September there were six Kings Cross diagrams to Newcastle and return each weekday, five Gateshead and two Heaton to London. York had three turns to London, Two of which returned on Parcels trains. No set pattern of engines existed at Kings Cross; Gateshead used Classes A1/3/4 with an occasional 'A2' whilst Heaton used 'A1s' exclusively, even borrowing one from Gateshead when short of power, rather than use an 'A2/3'.

An unusual locomotive class to bring a main line express into Kings Cross on Tuesday, 6 September 1950 was 'B12' 4-6-0 No 61553 of Grantham. It had replaced 'A3' No 60112 at Grantham, where no pilot was then maintained, and worked the 14-coach train unaided. 23min were lost between Grantham and Huntingdon and Kings Cross reached 50min late.

The timetable of 28 September 1951 brought the first signs of standardised departure times from Kings Cross. Scottish and Newcastle trains left on the hour and those to Leeds at 18min past. There were exceptions to this; the previous 12.20 'Northumbrian' to Newcastle was retimed at 12.18 and both the 'Tees Tyne' and 'Yorkshire' Pullmans retained their respective 16.45 and 17.30 departures. There were West Riding trains also at 15.45 and 15.50.

At the same time certain train sets remained in the platforms at Kings Cross where they were cleaned out in readiness for return northwards. Hitherto it had been practice for almost all main line trains to be worked out to Holloway, Bounds Green or Hornsey sidings between journeys. For instance the 11.35 arrival from Leeds formed the 13.18 departure whilst the incoming engine remained in the platform until released to enter the station loco yard for coaling prior to taking the 15.50. The unique Quintiple articulated set, built in 1921, and used on the 10.10 (later 10.15) from London to Leeds and 17.30 return each weekday until 1939, was in 1950 included in the 9.18 to Leeds and 14.57 return instead of 9.55 Leeds-London and 18.18 return as previously. Incidentally this set, retained its painted legend 'Kings Cross and Leeds'. At the latter end of World War 2 the set was stored in Arkwright Street, Nottingham shed.

Suburban train times in off-peak hours were also standardised. Hitchin and Cambridge line slows connected at Finsbury Park for Hertford line, and then generally ran fast to Hatfield. Departures for New Barnet were at 29 minutes past the hour and to Hatfield at 59, both serving all stations whilst Hertford departures from Kings Cross left at 54min past the hour. Similar arrangements applied in the reverse direction but connections from Hertford line at Finsbury Park were poor. Three weeks after the timetable commenced some amendments were made. The 17.55 Cambridge and Peterborough started at 17.52 calling at Finsbury Park, Welwyn North and all stations to Hitchin where the train divided. It had two engines; a New England 'A2/3' plus a Kings Cross 'B1' providing a novel sight when No 60533 *Happy Knight* appeared. In response to extended pressure from Potters Bar travellers a new train was introduced at 17.58 which called at Finsbury Park, Potters Bar and all stations to Welwyn Garden City. Gresley eight-coach bogie local set No 80 was specially refurbished for this duty and first class compartments restored. The set had a special diagram which took it to Hitchin each afternoon to return as an outer suburban train reaching Kings Cross about 17.13 to form the 17.58 which was soon dubbed 'The Pottersbarbarian', usual power was a London 'L1'. Kings Cross had acquired six of the class shortly before to replace 'B1s' on outer suburban duties as well as empty stock trains out to Bounds Green or Hornsey and a few single trip workings on locals to Hatfield and Hertford North. THey were not allowed into Broad Street until 1958. Slight alterations to the engine bays in Kings Cross yard made the use of 'L1' engines possible for ecs duties.

In addition to the six at Kings Cross (Nos 67792/3/6/7/9/67800), Hornsey also acquired four 'L1s' from Neasden in December 1950 (Nos 67749/56/7/61) for use on ecs duties in order to eliminate double-heading of 'N2' 0-6-2T then found necessary. However, they were not a great success for soon after No 67756 stalled on the Wood Green fly-over on 6 December and two weeks later another stalled in the same place when hauling only 12 corridors. Later, two 'L1s' were used to haul the empty 'Aberdonian' or one 'L1' and an 'N2'. All four 'L1s' left Hornsey in 1952.

During the Christmas period of 1950 and following weeks the GN line witnessed such scenes of congestion and confusion the like of which had never occurred in the previous hundred years. Staff problems, accentuated by the increased number of locomotives diagrammed to use Kings Cross Top Shed, caused long lines of locomotives to form in the entrance to the Goods Yard awaiting entry to the shed. At times a second line formed at Holloway South culminating in a maximum of 24 engines on Saturday 23 December. It was made up of many classes from 'J52' up to 'A1' and 'A4'.

During 1951 the elderly Ivatt 4-4-2T used on Alexandra Palace branch pull & push trains were replaced by some 'N7' 0-6-2T. For use on Ferme Park-Feltham transfer trips via Harringay curve four GE 'J20' 0-6-0 moved to Hornsey where they were also used as shunters in the yards at New Barnet, New Southgate and Wood Green tunnel sidings.

From 7 May 1951 the 14.00 Kings Cross-Edinburgh was named 'Heart of Midlothian' and composed of 13 new BR standard coaches. For a time the train was hauled to Newcastle by 'A1' No 60151 *Midlothian*.

During 1950-1 there had been so many complaints of poor timekeeping and excessive engine failures that the Locomotive Superintendent at Liverpool Street mobilised every Inspector under his control to ride on ECML trains with a view to pinpointing the reasons. Blame had already been placed by the operators on to motive power and vice versa so the atmosphere was not very cordial. The outcome of the exercise was a complete revision of engine diagrams to reduce long through runs in favour of out and home 'engine and men' duties. Only two through London-Newcastle turns remained; 'Tees-Tyne Pullman' each way by Kings Cross and two night sleepers worked by Gateshead both remained lodging turns. Both Kings Cross and Copley Hill retained two through workings as did York. On other trains engines changed at Peterborough or Grantham. Wholesale transfers of Pacifics were; two Grantham 'A4s' to Kings Cross; 10 'A1' and 8 'A3' from Kings Cross to Grantham which also got one 'A1' from Copley Hill whence five 'A3s' moved to Doncaster. Thus 'Top Shed' became exclusively an 'A4' depot with 19 there plus No 10000. The 'A3' were shared between Grantham and Doncaster and the Eastern Region 'A1s' were at Grantham (10), Copley Hill (11) and Ardsley (1). This latter was No 60144 to work a parcels due into Hornsey at 4.20 and returning with the 13.18 express from Kings Cross. To assist Grantham in handling their increased allocation a triangle for engine turning was laid down on the western side of the depot. They then had express duties to London (11), York (5) and one each to Leeds and Newcastle.

To improve locomotive running six Kings Cross 'A4s' were allocated to 12 No 1 link drivers on a regular basis and a similar arrangement applied with 'A1s' at Grantham. The result was immediately apparent in greatly improved timekeeping and reduction of failures.

GN 0-6-0ST had been the mainstay of shunting duties in the various goods yards near London together with certain cross-London transfer trips for some 75 years. In late 1951 a 'J50' 0-6-0T No 68949 ran trials with a new diesel shunter No 15004 on transfer trips between Ferme Park and Herne Hill. Next year 30 'J50' were sent to Hornsey displacing most of the saddle tanks except for a small number retained for trips to Poplar Dock where 'J50' were not permitted.

Other locomotive events included the appearance of 'B1' No 61379 on the Immingham-London through turn following its naming *Mayflower* at Boston in honour of the Pilgrim Fathers' connection with the Lincolnshire town. A LMS Class 4 2-6-0 No 43080 worked up from Peterborough with the stopping train due Kings Cross 17.05 on 4 August and returned north four days later with the Ashburton Grove refuse train.

At about 10.00 on 22 January 1952 a collision occurred in the Hotel Curve tunnel beneath Kings Cross. 'N2' No 69569 ran into the rear of the 9.54 local train to Hertford hauled by No 69492. The rear of local set No 75 was damaged and derailed. Clearance work was extremely difficult in the confined space of this tunnel.

The body of King George VI was conveyed by train from Wolferton to Kings Cross arriving at 14.45 on 11 February 1952. From Kings Lynn the engine used to haul the nine coaches was BR Standard Pacific No 70000 *Britannia*.

Other Standard Pacifics were seen on GN lines on 19/20 April when GE Cambridge line trains were diverted via Palace Gates, Hertford North and Hitchin during engineering work at Broxbourne. Nos 70009/10 were noted as well as 'K1' Nos 62017/58.

The first allocation of a diesel shunter in the Kings Cross district came in July with No 12112, soon followed by more at Hornsey and Kings Cross.

During the 11 week period of the 1952 summer timetable the 'Capitals Ltd' achieved its most

99
The Kings Cross station centenary exhibition, 1952. Gresley GNR first-class dining saloon No 3034, as specially restored for the occasion. *C. R. L. Coles*

100
A famous Top Shed partnership — driver E. Hailstone with 'A4' 4-6-2 No 60014 *Silver Link*. *E. Neve*

101
'C2' 4-4-2 No 990 and 'C1' 4-4-2 No 251 combine forces on the 17.00 Kings Cross-Peterborough North, north of Potters Bar, 16 September 1953.
Derrick A. Dant

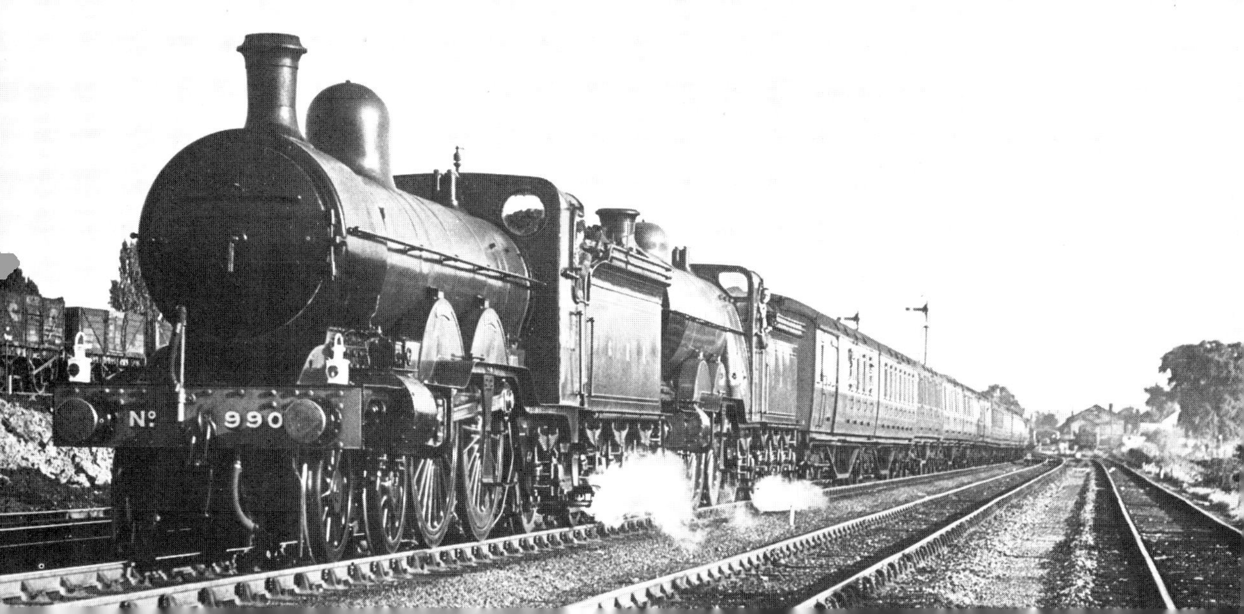

102
Unusual interloper. BR '4' 4-6-0 No 75034 of Bletchley shed at New Barnet with an SLS rail tour, 12 September 1963. Train composed of WR stock. *P. L. Melvill*

103
'WD' 2-8-0 No 90246 south of Greenwood with an up goods. *B. K. B. Green*

successful record for any postwar period. Only one engine failure was recorded. Remarkably that was by Haymarket's No 60027 *Merlin* — 'Magnificent *Merlin*' we called her. No failures were booked against any Top Shed 'A4s'. Altogether No 60027 completed 42 return trips that year.

The celebrate the centenary of opening the Great Northern London Terminus at Kings Cross an exhibition of engines, rolling stock and relics was held from October 13-18. Included were Stirling Single 4-2-2 No 1 of 1870, large Ivatt Atlantic No 251 of 1902 and Gresley 'A4' No 60022 *Mallard*.

A new fast express service from London to Bradford was put on in the winter of 1952. Leaving Kings Cross at 8.00 and calling only at Hitchin and Doncaster it reached Leeds at 11.31 and Bradford 11.55. Return was at 18.10 from Bradford to reach London at 22.05 with similar stops en route. At first 'A3' No 60056 *Centenary*, which had returned to Kings Cross shed by then, was used each way. London men worked to Doncaster, returning 'as required' and Leeds men brought the evening train up, also returning 'as required'. In the next timetable published the start from London was advanced to 7.50.

At long last the widening of the infamous Hadley Wood bottle-neck was authorised in 1953, estimated to cost £1¾ million. Three new tunnels were planned to accommodate the additional pair of tracks and Potters Bar station had to be rebuilt at an additional cost of £½m.

In honour of the new Queen, the Edinburgh non-stop was re-named the 'Elizabethan' and the schedule cut to 6hr 45min each way — the quickest so far. From London 'A4' No 60028 took the first run and No 60009 came up from Edinburgh. All enginemen wore special badges in blue with the name 'Elizabethan' on their overalls. The Scots crews transferred them to the lapels of their off-duty clothes. Great pride in the job was evident.

A privately organised special named the 'Plant Centenarian' ran from Kings Cross to Doncaster and back on Sunday 20 September 1953 hauled by the two preserved Ivatt Atlantics Nos 990 *Henry Oakley* and 251. The return from Doncaster was expertly handled by driver E. Hailstone and his own 'A4' No 60014 *Silver Link*. On the following Sunday the GN engines ran from Leeds and Doncaster to Kings Cross and No 60014 took the return. Prior to running the special to Doncaster the two Atlantics, in charge of drivers Hailstone (990) and Hoole (251) ran trial trips to Peterborough on the 17.00 semi-fast train from Kings Cross. Many regular GN line enthusiasts availed themselves of the opportunity to travel down to Hitchin on these days, recalling happy memories of previous times.

A Newcastle portion was added to the 7.50 'Bradford Flyer' in September. 'A1' No 60134 *Foxhunter* took the initial run to Leeds and Doncaster provided 'A3' No 60044 *Melton* to take the 6-coach Newcastle section forward.

During September and October when Kilsby tunnel on the LMR main line was under repair, nine LMR braked goods trains were diverted over ER lines, some travelling via Peterborough and Stamford and others via Grantham and Nottingham to Egginton Jct. At the London end trains gained ER metals via Harringay curve and also at Canonbury for those starting at Broad Street. Most were hauled by LMR Class 5 4-6-0s, but at least one 'Crab' 2-6-0 was noted. Again in January 1954 four similar diversions were made following derailment of the 'Royal Scot' at Watford.

Much excitement arose during the latter part of the summer when a dozen different 'B16' 4-6-0s appeared in London, mostly on goods trains or parcels but notably on 8 August when No 61420 took the 14.30 Leeds express from Kings Cross to Grantham and returned with the 'White Rose'. Ardsley 'J39' workings also increased with sightings on the 19.25 and 20.40 Parcels trains ex-London.

Early in 1954 the last large gantry near London still carrying GN somersault arms, south of Finsbury Park, was replaced by colour light signals.

Early in 1953 a start was made in cleaning the external brickwork of Kings Cross station, said to be the first time in 101 years. As a result the exterior took on a much improved image.

Following the disastrous collision at Harrow on the West Coast main line on 8 October 1952, the ER speeded up their experiments with Automatic Warning Systems. By April 1953 20 'A4' Pacifics, seven 'A3' and 11 'A1' had been equipped with apparatus together with 11 'V2' 2-6-2s. Full scale trials under the auspices of the Ministry of Transport were undertaken on 25 March using 'A4' No 60022 *Mallard* and again on 21 April with No 60034.

During March and April 1954 LMR 2-6-4T No 42374 spent some weeks on trial from Kings

Cross shed, at first working heavy empty stock out to Hornsey and later on Cambridge and Baldock stopping trains.

For the 1954 summer service the 'Elizabethan' was operated on a record 6hr 30min schedule over the $392\frac{3}{4}$ miles non-stop between London and Edinburgh except on Saturdays when an extra 37min were allowed. As usual the 'A4' Pacifics from Kings Cross and Haymarket performed well.

In order to improve running of certain important braked goods trains a new turn was included in Top Shed's No 1 link in August 1953. Going north on weekdays with the 2.30 (2.40MO) to York where the crew lodged and returned at 21.00 with the Aberdeen fish due Kings Cross at 2.05. Although the No 1 link had for many years incorporated a one-way trip on the same fish train from Grantham it was unknown for them to have goods workings from London. This did not last long because a special No 1A link was formed in 1954 to undertake another new lodge duty taking the 20.25 fast fitted goods to Hull returning next day with the 15.40 fish on which 'B1' engines were used. This link also took over the 02.30 York Lodge and another York turn leaving London at 16.05.

About this time also a Colwick engine and men lodge duty was introduced working the 21.00 fast goods from Colwick to London, lodging and returning light to Hitchin for the 17.20 thence to Colwick. Later this latter train started from Welwyn Garden City. 'K3' engines were used.

A new class appearing on outer suburban and Peterborough goods trains in August 1954 was BR standard Class 4 2-6-0 No 76039 of Neasden shed and at the same period another Fowler 2-6-4T No 42328 also appeared on outer suburban duties. These engines had been under repair at Kings Cross shed from it sub depot Neasden.

Many local enthusiasts travelled from Finsbury Park to Alexandra Palace on Saturday 3 July 1954 on the last passenger train to travel over the branch. Gaslit Gresley 8-coach set No 61 was headed by non-condensing 'N2' No 69519 on the 17.02 from Finsbury Park stopping at all five intermediate stations to Alexandra Palace $4\frac{1}{4}$ miles distant. A 3min late start encouraged the driver to some vigorous running and a severe snatch on the coupling when leaving Crouch End resulted in the drawbar fracturing when starting away from Highgate. It transpired the spare drawbars at each end of the train were unsuitable as replacements.

Fortunately the train was being followed by a Highbury Vale-Mill Hill coal train hauled by another 'N2' No 69526. This engine was detached from its wagons, having had their brakes pinned down, and used to propel the passenger train to the end of its journey while No 69519 ran light in front. On arrival at the terminus the propelling engine returned light to resume its coal train journey whilst No 69519 was attached to the undamaged end of set No 61 for the return to Finsbury Park, accompanied by exploding detonators.

The last surviving Ivatt 'J1' 0-6-0, No 65013, was withdrawn from Hitchin in November 1954 after a working life of 46 years. Latterly it had been employed on the weekend leave specials between Hitchin and Henlow on the former Midland Railway branch to Bedford. It was replaced on this work by a GE 'E4' 2-4-0 No 62785 which was some 12 years older!

In mid-November 1954 came a further development in locomotive power for the New England-Ferme Park coal trains. BR Class 9F 2-10-0 No 92030 arrived from Crewe and at once undertook a trial run hauling 45 loaded wagons, all vacuum braked. Departure from New England was at 5.50 and arrival at Ferme Park scheduled for 10.10 after a 54min halt at Hitchin South. In fact this trial was spoiled by fog because the train was diverted via the Hertford loop from Langley Jct. Afterwards trials continued with a quick turn-round at Hornsey to take 60 empty wagons back to New England on a 3hr 20min booking. Braking trials were conducted at various points en route both ways. Over the ensuing couple of months further '9Fs' were allocated to New England numbered 92031-42 to take over coal train duties from 'Austerity' 2-8-0s.

An outstanding change concerning inner suburban trains began in December when the first BR 5-coach compartment sets arrived to replace ageing Gresley gas-lit articulated 8-coach rakes.

104
LMS '4' 2-6-4T No 42374 at Greenwood on an up stopping train formed of a BR standard five-coach suburban set. April 1954. *Derrick A. Dant*

105
'A1' 4-6-2 No 60114 *W. P. Allen* on a diverted up Newcastle express passing Bayford, 13 September 1953. *E. Neve*

106
GNR clock on Platforms 3/4, Finsbury Park, 1953. *E. Neve*

107
'N1' 0-6-2T No 69435 passing Farringdon on the Widened Lines with a Hitchin-Brighton excursion. The 'N1' will work to New Cross Gate. *C. Hogg*

108
Alexandra Palace. 'N7' 0-6-2T No 69694 propels a push-pull train to Finsbury Park out of the station on 2 May 1953. *J. F. Henton*

109
A High Barnet-Southend excursion at East Finchley on 21 June 1953 behind 'N2' 0-6-2T No 69546.
H. Gordon Tidey

1956-1963

During the early weeks of 1955 the unique Class W1 4-6-4 No 60700 began regular work on Doncaster shed's weekday engine and men turn to London. Leaving Doncaster at 10.06 it reached Kings Cross at 12.52 and returned home with the 15.50 Leeds express. Whilst on the 15.50 on Thursday 1 September the engine was derailed at Westwood Jct. Shortly after starting away from Peterborough. Speed was then only about 20mile/h so little damage was sustained. The cause was later found to be a broken bogie frame.

Easter traffic over the ECML was reckoned to be the heaviest anywhere on BR. Maundy Thursday 1955 saw no less that 51 additional departures planned from Kings Cross and 41 arrivals. For the first time since the war there were no reports of engine failures south of Peterborough which tended to support the wisdom of changing engines at Peterborough or Grantham. A number of March 'V2s' were borrowed for the occasion. Perhaps the most curious timetable arrangement was for a Leeds relief leaving Kings Cross at 15.44 and stopping at Peterborough, Grantham and Doncaster running only five minutes ahead of the 15.49 ('West Riding' re-timed). The latter was non-stop to Wakefield hauled by 'A1' Pacific No 60130 which, in the event, passed the 15.44 ('W1' No 60700) at Peterborough.

In connection with proposals to adopt automatic warning system throughout BR, two Class 5 4-6-0s from Crewe arrived at Kings Cross for trials. First Stanier 'Black 5' No 44911 took the 14.05 'Cambridge Buffet Express' on 16 February, returning with the 17.21 ex-Cambridge. Next day it appeared on the same duty and BR Class 5 No 73071 took the 6.05 slow to Cambridge where it failed and was replaced on the 10.35 to London by 'B1' No 61287.

Additional lodging turns to Newcastle were introduced at Top Shed for the 1956 Summer service. Then the 10.00 'Flying Scotsman' was booked non-stop to Newcastle (SX) worked by Kings Cross engines and men who returned next day with the 'Tees-Tyne Pullman' arriving at 13.59 MSX, 14.30 ordinary train SO and 16.30 on Sunday. To work Monday's southbound 'Tees-Tyne' Kings Cross also went north on Sundays at 11.05. To work the 'Flying Scotsman' non-stop from Newcastle (SX) the engine and men off the 16.45 (SX) were used. To accommodate additional duties Kings Cross received 'A3' Pacifics Nos 60054 from Leicester and Nos 60055/66 from Doncaster, plus 'V2' Nos 60820/77 from Leicester and Doncaster.

Main line departures from Kings Cross on Saturdays were standardised at 0 and 40min past the hour to Newcastle or beyond, 18 and 52 for West Riding and 28 used for Hull and Scarborough. One exception to this was the absence of a 16.00 although there was a Newcastle relief at 15.52 instead of to the West Riding.

350HP diesel shunters began to arrive at Kings Cross and Hornsey in replacement of steam engines during January 1956. Four diesels Nos 13158-61 were seen at Hitchin en route to London on 30 January.

The 'Elizabethan' ran from 25 June to

110
BR '9F' 2-10-0 No 92040 takes an up coal train through Huntingdon North on 23 July 1959.
D. C. Ovenden

16 September 1956, still on a 6hr 30min schedule Monday-Friday and with 'A4' haulage. Week-end balancing duties, with one stop at Newcastle each way, were on the 9.0 from Kings Cross and 9.45 from Edinburgh (SO) and 10.00 ex-Kings Cross and 10.50 ex-Edinburgh (Sun). On 4 July No 60030 *Golden Fleece* was hastily requisitioned at Kings Crss to take the down non-stop but had to be removed at Newcastle with steaming troubles. This proved to be the only failure of the season. Floods in the Border country caused severe dislocation in late August when the 'Elizabethan' was diverted via Carlisle and Hawick with engine changes at Newcastle thus bringing Gateshead 'A4' No 60016 *Silver King* to London on 28 August. Matters had improved by 30 August when Haymarket's No 60011 *Empire of India* passed Newcastle 30min late but reached Kings Cross only 13min down. During the season Top Shed's No 60033 *Seagull* made 56 trips (26 successive) and Haymarket's No 60011 did one more (20 successive).

The winter Timetable starting on 17 September included some innovations. A new afternoon express service between London and Edinburgh was christened the 'Talisman'. Leaving each end at 16.00 it had a 6hr 40min schedule with one stop at Newcastle. Haulage was shared between Kings Cross and Gateshead sheds on a lodging basis. Going north M/W/F Kings Cross engine and men returned next day with the 7.50 ex-Newcastle whilst Gateshead, having reached Kings Cross on M/W/F took the 10.10 down on T/Th/S. Inaugural trips were made by 'A4' Nos 60025 *Falcon* and 60018 *Sparrow Hawk*. To give the down 'Talisman' a clear run, the 15.52 Kings Cross-Leeds was turned slow line from Potters Bar to Welwyn Garden City.

A distinctly unusual change involved the speeding up of the 15.15 Class C braked goods Kings Cross-Glasgow (the erstwhile 'Three-Forty Scotsman') which became non-stop to York in 288min and then fast to Newcastle reached around 22.30. At Newcastle a stop was made on the goods lines for engine changing and relief of the Kings Cross Top Link crew who lodged and returned home next morning at 10.00 ('Northumbrian'). For this new duty three 'A1' Nos 60149/56/7 moved from Grantham to Kings Cross in exchange for 'A3' Nos 60044/50/63 all of which had transferred earlier in the year from Neasden to Top Shed.

With the new goods lodge and the 'Talisman' and 'Tees-Tyne Pullman' Kings Cross operated three daily Newcastle turns (SX) and three on Sundays. Gateshead had two to London, arriving at 6.20 (7.10 Sun) returning at 22.15 same night and the 'Talisman' as stated above. To work the 10.10 on Mondays the 15.45 Newcastle-Kings Cross Sundays was used. The three Kings Cross 'A1s' soon undertook most of the Newcastle turns in conjunction with 'A4s' and early in 1957 the link was increased from 18 to 20 crews, nominally booked to regular engines. 'A4' Nos 60003/7/14/5/22/8/33/4 and 'A1' Nos 60149/56.

The down 'Flying Scotsman' reverted to New England engines and men who arrived in London at 7.40 with an Aberdeen night express before taking the 10.00 to Grantham and returning light to Peterborough. 'A2/3' No 60500 *Edward Thompson* was maintained in good condition for this duty.

Early signs of forthcoming dieselisation on passenger trains were seen in October 1956 when a two-car DMU consisting of BSO No E79063 and SO No E79279 arrived from Lincoln. It was used to train men from various ER depots. On Mondays the unit travelled from Stratford via Canonbury to Hadley Wood where the men lodged while undergoing tuition, and then made a number of trips between Baldock and Harston before returning to Hadley Wood at night. Training trips continued on Tuesdays to Fridays after which the unit returned to Stratford for servicing. It was stabled at New Barnet on Monday-Thursday nights.

An unusual sight on two days in February 1957 was 'A4' No 60028 hauling the complete 'Queen of Scots' Pullman train empty from Finsbury Park to Hitchin where the engine ran round and worked the train back to Kings Cross tender-first. Both engine and train later took up the normal public 12 noon departure. The special trials were to test the effect of the experimental aws system on Pullman stock.

Much interest was aroused about this time by frequent appearances of Scottish based Pacifics of all varieties on various parcels or fast goods trains between Doncaster and London. In this way many engines never previously seen in the south visited Kings Cross.

The first re-allocation of 'A4s' for about six years came in April 1957 when Nos 60003/8/10/30 moved to Grantham from Kings Cross. In consequence the corridor tender off No 60008 was attached to No 60021 in place of the latter's non--corridor. To make good this loss Top Shed received 'A1' Nos 60136/9 and 'A3s' Nos 60044/103 from Grantham plus 'A3' Nos 60039/59 from Leicester (GC)

A series of trials was conducted on certain through Newcastle duties using 'A3s' to determine their suitability for such work. In view of reduced loads the results were favourable and much more use was made of the older Pacifics henceforth.

For a large number of East Coast observers, an auspicious occasion came on 5 April 1957 when driver Hailstone made his last runs before retirement. Regular lunchtime watchers were able to witness his departure at 14.00 with the 'Heart of Midlothian' as far as Peterborough. Later a far greater number awaited arrival of the Glasgow express on which the deservedly famous team of Hailstone and *Silver Link* had converted a $2\frac{1}{2}$min late start from Peterborough into an 8min early arrival. Over the years from 1950 when Hailstone first appeared, completely unknown, in the top link at Kings Cross, many of us established a friendly relationship with this dedicated engineman.

Because of deteriorating punctuality there were some decelerations in the 1957 summer timetable but an attempt to improve running was reflected by no less than five booked non-stop runs between London and Newcastle Monday-Thursday. Six Kings Cross engine and men diagrams operated to Newcastle at 7.45, 10.00, 15.15 (Goods), 16.00, 16.50 and 19.45 (sleeper FX). They also shared the 'Elizabethan' with Haymarket as usual on alternate days. To accommodate the extra work 'A1s' Nos 60125/58 and 'A3' No 60110 moved to London from Grantham and 'A3' No 60066 from Doncaster. The No 1 link at Top Shed was increased to 28 crews and the eminently successful system of double manning regular engines was abandoned. Gateshead retained their two lodge turns to London, arriving at 6.40 and 22.45 ('Talisman') and returning at 22.15 and 10.10 (next day) respectively.

The main innovation was a new 'Morning Talisman' at 7.45 from London and 7.30 from Edinburgh taking 6hr 45min each way; the train sets forming the 16.00 'Afternoon Talisman' services from each end. Except on the 'Elizabethan' Kings Cross Class 'A1', 'A3' and 'A4' Pacifics indiscriminately whilst Gateshead normally used an 'A4' on the 'Afternoon Talisman' and 'A1' Nos 60154/5 on the night trains.

Further revolutionary changes took place in September 1957 of which the most notable was extension of the 'Morning Talisman' (re-named 'The Fair Maid') to Perth via the Forth Bridge and Dunfermline and a similar extension of the 'Heart of Midlothian'. The latter's departure from London was advanced to 13.00 and it was routed via Falkirk, Larbert and Stirling, thus becoming the first ever through train between Kings Cross and Stirling. The 'Flying Scotsman' was accelerated by 37min to Edinburgh, still non-stop to/from Newcastle (SX). The 'Aberdonian', composed entirely of sleeping cars was re-timed to leave at 22.15

111
A London terminus with two Gresley Pacifics — Marylebone on 12 May 1956. 'A4' 4-6-2 No 60014 *Silver Link* on the Ian Allan 'Pennine Pullman' excursion to Sheffield and Manchester. Alongside is 'A3' 4-6-2 No 60063 *Isinglass* with the 10.00 to Manchester. The author is immediately right of No 60014.
E. Neve collection

112
The down 'Talisman' at Potters Bar behind 'A4' 4-6-2 No 60013 *Dominion of New Zealand*, 1957. *J. F. Aylard*

instead of 19.00. A new 19.45 from London conveyed sleepers for Aberdeen and Fort William also through coaches to Elgin. The 'Night Scotsman' was put back from 22.15 to 23.35, also made up of sleepers only. The chief aim of the latter alterations, on which similar arrangements applied in the reverse direction, was to provide much lighter and faster trains than before.

Other changes included starting the early West Riding express at 8.00 and adding a Hull portion in place of one to Newcastle for which place an additional 9.00 train was put on. New semi-fasts left at 8.20 and 18.35 to Doncaster and 14.10 to York and Hull.

These changes occasioned another mass movement of Pacifics. The four 'A4s' sent to Grantham in April all returned to Kings Cross together with 'A1' Nos 60113/9/22/8/44, thus bringing their stud up to 40 Pacifics. But Nos 60113/44 moved away to Doncaster shortly after. It was difficult to understand this heavy concentration at Top Shed and the severe reduction in Grantham's stud where maintenance facilities were superior to those in London at the time, and the enginemen had made a notable contribution to performance in the previous six years. Grantham retained their engine and men duty to Newcastle, working the 9.00 ex-Kings Cross and 'Heart of Midlothian' return but used other shed's engines on most of their turns.

Accelerations had been applied to the principal fast braked goods trains from Kings Cross. The famous Scotch goods departure was advanced to 15.05 for a non-stop run to York (Skelton) 189 miles; a similar run was made by the 2.30 goods whilst the 16.30 ran non-stop to Selby. The down 20.20 Hull goods ran fast to Hougham loop but its return fish train balance was non-stop between Hull and New England. All these trains continued as lodging turns by Kings Cross as described earlier.

Late in 1957 BR Standard Class 5 4-6-0 Nos 73157-9 were transferred from Neasden to Kings Cross in exchange for 'V2' Nos 60855/76/7 and were seen on such duties as 6.53 Cambridge slow passenger, 16.39 Broad Street-Baldock and 20.20 Hull goods. No 73158 also appeared on Newmarket Race specials. The BR '9F' 2-10-0 began to appear on some braked goods.

Early in February 1958 a two-car DMU from Derby ran trials with aws over the GN main line. Starting at Derby the unit ran via Nottingham and Grantham to Kings Cross (arrive 13.14, depart 13.45). It had a 120min schedule to Grantham on the return.

Although original plans envisaged that the first examples of new 2,000hp diesel-electric locomotives allotted to the Eastern Region would be used in East Anglia, it was decided later to put some on the ECML. The first example seen was on 9 April 1958 when No D200 worked a special trial conveying seven coaches from Doncaster to Welwyn Garden City and back. This was followed by No D201 arriving at Hornsey, where temporary diesel servicing facilities had been provided in part of the former steam shed. The new unit made trial runs to Royston and Sheffield, then worked crew training trips, before taking the first diesel hauled 'Flying Scotsman' to Newcastle on 21 June.

Due to arrears of maintenance an 'A5' 4-6-2T No 69824 was taken from store at Lincoln to work ecs and occasional outer suburban passenger trains from Kings Cross whilst GE 0-6-0T No 68626 (Class 'J69') and 68638 ('J68') arrived at Hornsey from Peterborough and Hitchin respectively to shunt in the Ferme Park Yards.

Apart from new diesel types, mentioned later, there was a great deal of change in the use of '9F' 2-10-0s. On 8 May 1958 there was a special trial worked by one of these standard engines from Doncaster to Kings Cross goods. It left Doncaster at 9.00 with 40 loaded 16ton vacuum fitted mineral wagons and was booked into Kings Cross at 13.32 with a 2min stop at Peterborough for crew change. For most of the way this train travelled on the main lines. During the summer months '9Fs' appeared on passenger trains, notably in August when Nos 92036 and 92184 were on Kings Cross-Peterborough slows over the Bank Holiday period but even more remarkable was the use of No 92195 on the 15.00 express for Newcastle on 15 August and No 92184 next day took the 13.52 Leeds express as far as Grantham to return with the up 'Heart of Midlothian' on which it was timed to a maximum of 90mile/h on the descent from Stoke summit. Nos 92187/8 were allocated to Grantham shed and frequently worked the 5.15 parcels out of Kings Cross.

Other unusual use of locomotives from distant sheds included several instances of March based 'K1s' on Cambridge-Kings Cross passenger trains and associated workings while 'B16' 4-6-0s from York were prevalent on braked goods. Newly outshopped 'Britannias' from Doncaster Works were appropriated for GN line duties during August: No 70003 took the 11-18 Kings Cross-Hull on 23 August and No 70037 was on an up parcels. Five days later No 70041 brought up the Perth car sleeping train.

For the 1958 summer timetable the No 1 link at Top Shed was increased to an unprecedented total of 40 sets of men — a far cry from 30 years earlier when there were only six. Such a large influx of comparatively inexperienced men, particularly firemen, coupled with poor coal and abandonment of regular manning had a detrimental effect on timekeeping. Maintenance could not keep pace with demands — instanced by recourse to 'A3s' to cover express passenger long distance diagrams. A more encouraging feature of the summer was that Grantham regained a measure of express passenger engine diagrams, including the 9.40 Kings Cross-Newcastle throughout.

Away from the main line duties, Hornsey had a newcomer in the shape of 'J94' 0-6-0ST No 68033 for trials on transfer trips to Poplar Dock, hitherto the preserve of elderly GN saddle tanks. In time more 'J94s' arrived and the long reign, spanning some 75 years, of the GN saddle tanks was ended. During this period much trouble was being experienced with the 'L1' 2-6-4T used on outer suburban passenger and empty stock duties. They were prone to severe slipping on the gradients through the tunnels and unable to steam properly when handling some long non-stop outer suburban trains, notably the 17.39 to Baldock usually patronised by some of the ER 'top brass'. As a solution the second engine of the 17.52 Cambridge/Peterborough train was switched to the 17.39 as far as Hitchin and two BR Standard '4' 2-6-4Ts Nos 80103/37 were received on loan at Kings Cross. Coincidentally restrictions were lifted on the working of 'L1s' into Broad Street and the class became more common on inner suburban duties such as the 17.26 and 17.36 ex-Broad Street.

With this unusual steam activity as a background the arrival of more English Electric Type 4 2,000hp units at Hornsey, numbered D206-9, was followed by their appearance on a number of express duties in lieu of steam. About the same time came the announcement of the order for 22 3,300hp 'Deltics' in replacement of 55 steam locomotives. Nevertheless modifications to Pacifics were proceeding and in June 'A3' No 60055 *Woolwinder* made its debut fitted with a Kylchap double blast pipe and chimney. In November the same modification to all the 'A4s' was completed while conversion of the 'A3s' was completed in January 1960. In the closing weeks of the 1958 summer service it was obvious that the depots were hard pressed to find suitable steam power to cover daily diagrams, with failures occurring and engines being borrowed from other depots. So bad was the maintenance position that 40 engines were laid off and the situation was considered to have deteriorated to the low level reached between 1949-51. An example lay in the record of 'A4' No 60014 *Silver Link*, which in the 12 months subsequent to driver E. Hailstone's retirement in April 1957, ran 30,000 fewer miles than in the last 12 months of his distinguished partnership with that engine. Even so, some fine running was recorded with Pacifics during this period, such as 'A4' No 60021 taking the 245ton 8.20 from Kings Cross over the 27.0miles between Hitchin and Huntingdon start to stop in 20min 46sec, attaining 99mile/h at Tempsford, and averaging 93.1mile/h over the 19 miles between Arlesey and Offord.

For the winter 1958 timetable five diagrams were produced for the EE Type 4 diesels, each requiring between 4,220 and 4,689 miles weekly. For publicity reasons the newly introduced 'Master Cutler' all-Pullman train at 07.20 from Sheffield and 19.20 from Kings Cross plus the mid-day workings of the stock to Sheffield at 11.20 and back at 15.20 were diagrammed exclusively for diesel haulage. In addition to the Sheffield workings the five diesels had several duties over the ECML to Newcastle and elsewhere. Interestingly the unit taking the 19.20 Pullman to Sheffield on Monday to Thursday nights, worked the 00.35 Sheffield-Annesley Class H goods, returning on the 4.44 Class C from Annesley on Tuesday-Friday.

The new diesel diagrams left Top Shed's 27 '8P' ('A1/A4') Pacifics with only 10 daily duties, with one extra on Fridays. The 11 '7P' Pacifics fared rather better, having five duties daily, with an extra one on Fridays. Although all five Type 4 diesels were reputedly available by early October, one of the diesel diagrams was being steam operated in part and the situation was worse in mid-November, many failures occurring which resulted in the use of Pacifics on the 'Master Cutler'. Because there was no suitable steam power at either Sheffield or Retford which could be substituted for failed diesels it was arranged that the connecting train

69577

THE HEART OF MIDLOTHIAN
60014

113
Trouble at Platform 16, Kings Cross with a train off the Widened Lines means that this down suburban train is double headed by 'N2' 0-6-2T No 69577 and 'N2' 0-6-2T No 69543, entering Finsbury Park, 16 June 1957. *J. F. Aylard*

114
Driver E. Hailstone on his final run, 4 April 1957, with 'A4' 4-6-2 No 60014 *Silver Link* leaving Kings Cross on the down 'Heart of Midlothian'. *Derrick A. Dant*

115
Welwyn North station in the 1950s.

116
'N2' 0-6-2T No 69595 crosses the Hertford line viaduct at Wood Green with empty stock, 14 September 1957. *B. K. B. Green*

from Doncaster to Retford, not normally requiring high power, should be Pacific hauled to provide emergency cover for the up 'Master Cutler'.

Apart from the new Sheffield Pullman service there were few alterations in 1958 timetables but both the 'Fair Maid' and 'Heart of Midlothian' ceased serving Perth after 12 September. The 'Aberdonian' reverted to its long-standing 19.30 departure from Kings Cross (FX) or 19.45 (FO). A development in fish trains was to equip the 12.30 Aberdeen-Kings Cross with newly designed vans running on roller bearings and carrying a blue spot 15in in diameter to distinguish them from 'common user' vans. The train reached London at 2.05, worked from York by the Kings Cross 1A link and the empties returned north mid-morning.

Towards the end of 1958 there were deliveries of Type 2 diesels, intended to replace the 'N2' and 'L1' steam engines on Kings Cross suburban services. By April 1959 three different types were in service: the BRCW 1,160hp D53xx series, the NBL 1,000hp D61xx series and the EE 1,100hp D59xx series 'Baby Deltics'. Even more notable was the arrival on 19 January of the prototype 3,300hp 'Deltic' for month-long trials. May 1959 was the intended date for complete dieselisation of all suburban services employing a mixture of DMUs and locomotives, working to accelerated timings. In July, however, it was reported that although Hornsey had 46 diesel units to cover 34 diagrams the shed was obliged to prepare a steam engine for every diagram in view of the prevalence of failures.

At the end of April 1959 six 'A1s' went to Doncaster from Kings Cross shed which received three double chimney 'A3s' in exchange. At the same time the use of Pacifics on diesel diagrams increased. For example, 'A1' No 60156 made a return trip to Newcastle with the 10.00 down and 17.00 back, left for Leeds at 4.00 next morning and left for Kings Cross at 12.30: a total of 910 train miles in 30hr 30min. There was adequate proof that the fitting of double chimneys to the Gresley Pacifics was reaping dividends for so successful were these modifications that the engines were running an additional 20-25,000 miles between works repairs. Whereas 'A3s' had been regarded as second class power during the early 1950s they now became 'star' performers such as No 60061 *Pretty Polly* which was recorded as working the up 'Flying Scotsman' through from Newcastle to London, 268.3 miles in exactly 268min inclusive of two pws, three signal checks and one dead stand before Finsbury Park.

Of all the many notable performances set up by Gresley Pacifics during 1959, one reached heights destined never to be repeated. To celebrate their Golden Jubilee the Stephenson Locomotive Society chartered a special train to Doncaster and back on Saturday 23 May. The chosen engine was 'A4' No 60007 *Sir Nigel Gresley* ably handled by driver W. Hoole and fireman A. Hancox. Brilliant sunshine throughout the day enhanced the outstanding work by engine and crew and made it a memorable occasion for every admirer of the Gresley 'A4s'. Going down, the summit of the Northern Heights at Potters Bar was topped at 59mile/h and Hitchin (31.9 miles) was passed in 32min 4sec at 93mile/h. Shortly afterwards a speed of 101mile/h was reached and the fast 55min booking from Kings Cross to Huntingdon was bettered by 3min. After a slack at Werrington Junction the engine was opened out to some purpose which culminated in a record 82mile/h at Stoke summit. Returning from Doncaster, the schedule allowed an exacting 144min for the 156.0 miles to Kings Cross inclusive of three speed restrictions and the customary 20mile/h service slack through Peterborough. A 2min late start provided scope for time recovery which was achieved before Newark. Onwards to Stoke the engine was kept hard at it, passing the summit a few seconds early at 75mile/h. After this all eyes were glued to mileposts and stop watches in anticipation of a high maximum down the famous bank. Before Little Bytham speed had reached the magic 'hundred' and shortly after 112 was attained. After easing through Huntingdon the engine was opened out once more until near Tempsford 100mile/h was again reached, thereby treating the participants to their third 'hundred' of the day. After a superb climb up to Stevenage, topped at a minimum of 76mile/h, Kings Cross was reached over 6min early on schedule. To demonstrate their excellence the same engine and crew working the up 'Northumbrian' of 430ton from Newcastle to London during the following week produced a recorded 108mile/h down Stoke bank.

Throughout the summer of 1959 'A4s' continued to deputise on diesel diagrams, at the same time maintaining a commendable performance on the non-stop 'Elizabethan'. Top Shed's star performer was No 60028 which made 24 return trips and five singles while Haymarket's No 60027 ran 31 return trips during the season. Throughout the autumn only the outstanding performances of Pacifics enabled the East Coast services to operate, for the diesels continued to disappoint. During the three weeks ended 20 December only twice were diesels seen on the 10.00 to Newcastle and 17.00 return. 'A4' No 60030 worked this turn on 13 out of 18 days and also did two return trips to Leeds, totalling 9,018 miles in three weeks. The year ended with the first 'A3' withdrawal, that of No 60104 *Solario*.

If 1959 was not an auspicious year for the Eastern Region's new diesels, then 1960 proved little better. On the suburban front it was already clear that the NBL Type 2 were not capable of any consistent work while the BRCW Type 2s were too heavy for use on the cross-London transfer goods via Snow Hill so both types were replaced by Brush Type 2s. The main line diesels were faring little better for the fastest East Coast trains observed during the four weeks ended 5 March the 10.00 was headed by 'A4s' on 13 days out of 17 sightings while the 17.35, seen 18 times had a diesel on only three occasions — 'A3s' or 'A4s' being in charge otherwise. Some fine performances were recorded behind Pacifics acting as main line pilots instanced when the 'Morning Talisman' stopped at Darlington where the pilot, No 60071 *Tranquil*, took over from a Type 4. Leaving 20min late and suffering one pws had a dead stand at Offord, the 232.3 miles to London were covered in 210min with an 'on time' arrival. During May 1960 Top Shed's Pacifics continued to make news. 'A4' No 60022 *Mallard* headed the 10.00 to Newcastle and returned the same day, normally on the 17.00 up, on seven successive occasions between 7 and 13 May and notched up 3,752 miles. 'A3' No 60061 *Pretty Polly* was conspicuous on a similarly exacting turn taking the 'Morning Talisman' to Newcastle and returning with the 'Afternoon Talisman'. In four weeks No 60061 amassed 11,000 miles. It must not be overlooked that Gateshead's two roller bearing 'A1s', Nos 60154/5 also put in some very high mileages working the nightly lodging turn to London and back often being borrowed by Top Shed for a trip to Peterborough or Grantham in between.

In March 1961 the first production 'Deltic', No D9001, was delivered to the ER, followed at regular intervals by others. All 22 were in service by April 1962 allocated as follows: Finsbury Park Nos D9001/3/7/9/12/5/8/20; Gateshead Nos D9002/5/8/11/4/7; Haymarket Nos D9000/4/6/10/3/6/9/21.

'Britannia' Pacifics, made redundant on GE lines, were transferred to Immingham shed, intended for use on the two daily passenger duties to London in place of 'B1s' but such was the Pacifics' condition that only one was in service. Meanwhile Hitchin shed closed on 12 June.

One of the highlights of 1961 was the provision of three special trains to York, returning from Malton, on the occasion of the Duke of Kent's wedding on 8 June. All three were taken by Top Shed 'A4s' turned out in splendid fashion. No 60028 was on the Royal train, Nos 60003/15 taking the others.

For the 1961 summer service the Type 4 cyclic diagrams were abandoned and three of the units transferred to the GE lines. Two were retained at Finsbury Park depot, now in full use as the principal GN line diesel servicing for use on the 'Sheffield Pullman' workings and 22.30 to Newcastle returning with the 'Tees-Tyne Pullman'. Only 30% of the express passenger trains were scheduled for steam haulage although in the event the percentage was much greater. On an August day no less than 85% were steam hauled through Hadley Wood. Albeit 1961 was the last summer of significant steam operation.

Official intentions were for 'Deltics' to power the 'Elizabethan' non-stop between London and Edinburgh but availability and crewing problems prevented this. So for the last time the 'A4s' were used and no effort was spared by both Top Shed and Haymarket to produce a good showing. Bearing in mind the run-down in steam maintenance, and disorganisation resulting from diesel availability problems, the result was really creditable in that only one failure was recorded. This was on 31 August when No 60030 was removed from the down train at Newcastle with injector trouble. Five Kings Cross engines were employed on the non-stop, Nos 60014/22/8/30/3, while Haymarket used only three, Nos 60009/24/31. Pride of place went to No 60009 which completed 14 consecutive journeys between 13 August and 9 September on which day she worked the last up non-stop. The final down train was taken by No 60022 *Mallard*. The schedule was 6hr 35min — 5min slower than the best postwar booking of 6hr 30min 1954-6 but

117
A record of the ill-fated vacuum braked train of 16ton mineral wagons, loaded with coal for Top Shed, and approaching Finsbury Park behind BR '9F' 2-10-0 No 92174 on 8 May 1958. *J. F. Aylard*

118
Widening work in progress at Greenwood, April 1959. 'A4' 4-6-2 No 60026 *Miles Beevor* on the up 'Aberdonian' sleeping car train. *J. F. Aylard*

119
An up fitted goods passes Woolmer Green behind Kings Cross 'V2' 2-6-2 No 60814 in lined green livery, 11 July 1958. *E. R. Wethersett/Ian Allan Library*

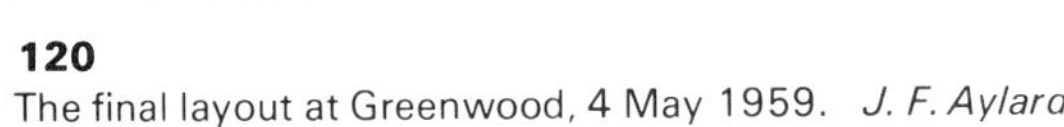

120
The final layout at Greenwood, 4 May 1959. *J. F. Aylard*

121
Driver Bill Hoole in the cab of 'A4' 4-6-2 No 60007 *Sir Nigel Gresley* at Kings Cross on the occasion of the famed SLS Jubilee run of July 1959. *E. Neve*

122
'J6' 0-6-0 No 64175 on an engineer's train on the up slow line at Greenwood, July 1959. *Derek Cross*

an improvement on the best prewar 7hr. Allowing for the eight-year break during the war the Edinburgh non-stop had operated for 25 summer seasons between 1928-61, always capably handled the Gresley Pacifics 'A1', 'A3' or 'A4' and their crews who took great pride in this prestige working.

Deliveries of 'Deltics' were expected to greatly aid the elimination of steam from the winter timetable of 1961/2, but no great changes were made in schedules. Thirteen new diagrams were produced to cover the entire East Coast service with many through turns to and from Edinburgh although a proportion of the Leeds trains were to be steam hauled. In the event so many steam substitutions were necessary that it is impossible to record them all. The type 4s based at Leeds Neville Hill were booked to work the 'Queen of Scots' Pullmans but were frequently replaced by Pacifics from the same shed — by then unusual at Kings Cross. To cover ecs duties in the Kings Cross district six 'N2' and four 'L1' tanks emerged from retirement. Ardsley 'A3s' were consistently seen on the express goods duties to London, particularly two erstwhile Gateshead favourites Nos 60070 *Gladiateur* and 60077 *The White Knight* which 30 years earlier had entertained the GN line observers when working the 'Flying Scotsman' diagrams.

In mid-January 1962 the three Neville Hill Type 4 diagrams to London were abandoned due to poor availability. This resulted in an assortment of Pacifics working the 'Queen of Scots' both ways, including another firm favourite of past times, No 60073 from Gateshead. Amongst the continuing visits of Scottish Region Pacifics after overhaul at Doncaster was one by 'A4' No 60031, with a St Rollox (65B) shed plate on 30 March — having replaced a 'Deltic' at Doncaster on the up 'White Rose'. On 15 March Dr Beeching travelled to Newcastle on the 09.00 from Kings Cross which was headed by 'A4' No 60007. Was this a diplomatic blunder or just a gentle hint from the motive power people?

Following repeated trouble the 'Baby Deltics' were taken out of service pending a decision on their future. A sad note was struck on 26 May when the last 'N2' left Kings Cross for storage at Peterborough, bringing to an end their association from early 1921 with the Kings Cross suburban duties.

Saturday 2 June 1962 saw 'A4' No 60022 *Mallard* depart from Kings Cross at 8.00 on what was billed as the last non-stop steam run to Edinburgh. All went well until just south of Berwick where the special was stopped by signal thanks to a hot box on a preceding train. Prior to 1961 when used on the 'Elizabethan' non-stop to Edinburgh several trivial happenings had frequently arisen to forestall a non-stop run. So in 1962 *Mallard's* jinx had struck again!

In 1962 there was no booked non-stop running between London and Edinburgh since a stop was inserted at Newcastle in the 'Elizabethan' schedule, mainly for crew changing purposes. With all 22 'Deltics' nominally available, 20 diagrams were produced for the winter 1962/3 timetable. Surprisingly, there were still 17 Pacific diagrams at Top Shed: eight 'A4' and nine 'A3'. On 8 October 1962 the first Brush 2,750hp Type 4 made its debut, heralding more speedy removal of steam, particularly as these locomotives were to prove much more reliable than their predecessors. On 30 October there was a welcome sight of 'B16/3' No 61420 on an up goods. The daily 16.12 York braked goods from Kings Cross had by then been taken over by 'A3s' from 'V2s' the latter increasingly relegated to unfitted services. On 8 November the Cleethorpes-Kings Cross turns worked by Immingham were allocated Type 3 diesels based on Sheffield Darnall.

Early in January 1963 came the dreaded news that five Kings Cross 'A4s' Nos 60003/14/28/30/3 had been withdrawn. Although it had been mooted that *Silver Link* might be purchased for preservation, it was cut up soon after, to the utter despair of every Gresley supporter. By contrast it also became known that 'A3' No 60103 *Flying Scotsman* had been purchased by Mr A. F. Pegler and would make its last run on the 13.15 from Kings Cross on 14 January. An event which brought out the Gresley supporters, and many others too, to pay their respects to the old favourite.

From 1957 there had been progressive movement of 'A1' Pacifics from Kings Cross to Doncaster as well as some withdrawals causing a slight increase in the number of 'V2' substitutions for failed diesels. At Easter 1963 over half the principal trains were steam hauled and at Whitsun similar conditions prevailed.

It was the firm intention to eliminate steam south of Peterborough with the start of the 1963 summer

123
Little Wymondley, south of Hitchin. 'L1' 2-6-4T No 67744 with an up outer suburban train composed of BR non-corridor stock, 14 July 1959.
E. R. Wethersett/Ian Allan Library

124
Hitchin's 'J15' 0-6-0 No 65479 arrives at its home station with the up Henlow Camp leave train on 11 June 1960. A 'B1' 4-6-0 stands on Hitchin shed.
J. E. K. Chambers

timetable, all passenger duties being dieselised. Kings Cross shed was closed after the evening of 15 June. Prior to this 10 of the remaining Top Shed Pacifics were seen at work and in the final week 'A4' No 60008 completed four return trips to Newcastle. During the evening of Friday 14 June 10 out of 16 main line passenger and goods trains were steam hauled. For the last Saturday Top Shed turned out 'A4' Nos 60017/25 for the 9.05 Newcastle and 09.20 'White Rose' to Leeds, followed by 'A3' Nos 60061/3 on the 10.10 Leeds and 11.15 Scarborough respectively. The final scheduled steam working (to Leeds) on 16 June was taken by 'A1' No 60158 of Doncaster at 22.45. Prior to these notable events, two unusual LMR engines were seen at Kings Cross, Holbeck 'Jubilee' No 45597 brought in a special from Bradford on 8 June and next day Camden 'Duchess' Pacific No 46245 took a charter special to Doncaster and back.

With the closure of Top Shed its 11 'A4s' were transferred to New England, displacing 'A3s' sent to Grantham where they were joined by the surviving Kings Cross 'A3s'. The New England 'A2s' and four other 'A3s' were condemned.

Attempts to banish steam on principal workings to London were not successful, causing difficulties for control and shed staffs admonished to remove steam locomotives from southbound trains at Peterborough. On 6 July a special steam train was allowed to operate from Kings Cross to York and return, billed as a last main line steam working, and named 'Mallard Commemorative Rail Tour' by the LCGB organisers. 'A4' No 60007 took this train via Hitchin, Cambridge, Ely, March and Lincoln to York, returning direct to London. The return journey of 188$\frac{1}{4}$ miles was allowed 197min but took only 185$\frac{3}{4}$min gross, estimated at 166min net. A speed of 102mile/h was attained on the descent from Stoke.

Down to the end of 1963 there were a considerable number of steam workings into London, no less than 57 in October and over 40 recorded in December, including 'A3' No 60063 on the up 'Northumbrian' on 9 December. On the same day came what was to prove the very last steam worked 'Flying Scotsman' when 'A3' No 60106 *Flying Fox* was put on this train at York following a diesel failure and worked through to Kings Cross. Fate decreed that the run was not to be one for the record book in view of five signal checks, five pws and two dead stands to relight the headlamps.

Apart from the matter of extensive steam engine utilisation during the first years of dieselisation, there were a number of timetable changes from the winter 1961-2 issue. On 14 'Deltics' could be made available regularly so the main alterations came in overnight sleeper train schedules and day West Riding and Newcastle business services. For example the 7.45 Kings Cross-Leeds 'West Riding' was cut to 3hr 9min overall and the 7.30 from Leeds to a level 3hr reaching London at 10.30. The 'Yorkshire Pullman' had its departure put back to 17.25 and a substantial 30 minutes cut from the Kings Cross-Doncaster run. The 7.50 ex-Newcastle was booked non-stop from Darlington to London in 3hr 28min (67mile/h average) and took 4hr 15min overall from Tyneside. Apart from the 11.50 'Queen of Scots' and 12.20 'Northumbrian' there were hourly departures from Kings Cross to Newcastle from 8.00 until 16.00. In the next timetable (18 June 1962) there were six weekday fast timings of 6hr between London and Edinburgh on the 9.30 'Elizabethan', 10.00 'Flying Scotsman' and 16.00 'Afternoon Talisman' and their up counterparts. Because of the impracticability of crews travelling through between London and Edinburgh on the 'Deltic' hauled 'Elizabethan', a brief stop was made at Newcastle to change men. The 'Heart of Midlothian' once more reverted to a 14.00 departure from Kings Cross and 13.30 from Edinburgh while the 'Tees-Tyne Pullman' had stops inserted at York and made an all-time British start-to-stop record of 35min over the 44.1 miles Darlington-York. Other accelerations were made in night trains to take into account the 530ton 'Deltic' limit applicable to them.

Generally the arctic weather of early 1963 added to the motive power difficulties, steam appearing on many Kings Cross suburban workings as well as on the main line.

Major changes were made in GN main line goods and coal working in April 1963 by which time sufficient Type 4 Brush 2,750hp units were in service to implement a comprehensive scheme. The diesels could take 75 wagons on Class 4 (fully fitted) trains compared with 65 allowed for Type 4 or steam locomotives. This enabled some combination of traffic to destinations beyond York and a reduction in the total trains operated. One victim of this revision was the Kings Cross-Hull fitted goods, worked for several years by Top Shed 'B1s'.

125
Top Shed's immaculately groomed 'A4' 4-6-2 No 60032 *Gannet* backs on to the down 'Elizabethan' at Kings Cross on 14 June 1960. *J. F. Aylard*

126
Haymarket 'A4' 4-6-2 No 60027 *Merlin* leaves Kings Cross with the down 'Elizabethan' on 15 June 1960 — the first down run that summer with a Haymarket engine. *J. F. Aylard*

127
An up parcels train passes Oakleigh Park behind 'A2/3' 4-6-2 No 60520 *Owen Tudor* in September 1960. *Derek Cross*

Another notable feature was introduction of a 7* scheme for loaded coal trains between New England and Ferme Park on which the Type 4s could take up to 90 loaded wagons on 3hr schedules. This enabled six up trains from New England to be cancelled and four down empties from Ferme Park with beneficial results to line occupation.

128
Fitted with double chimney, 'A3' 4-6-2 No 60103 *Flying Scotsman* makes good progress past Oakleigh Park with the down 'Yorkshire Pullman' in the summer of 1960. *Derek Cross*

129
An example of a North Eastern Region 'A3' working at the southern end of the GN main line. Gateshead's 'A3' 4-6-2 No 60060 *The Tetrarch* with an up fitted goods south of Potters Bar, 14 May 1960. *K. L. Cook*

130
'N2s' saw some work on station pilot duties at Peterborough North at the finish of their lives. No 69513 at the north end of the station, May 1961. *G. D. King*

131
Kings Cross 'V2' 2-6-2 No 60817, fitted with a double chimney, takes a down parcels train away from Hadley North Tunnel on 13 June 1961. *Derek Cross*

132
Peterborough North as it was. 'A4' 4-6-2 No 60025 *Falcon* eases an up Leeds express through the station on 17 February 1962. *P. H. Wells*

133
Immingham's 'Britannia' 4-6-2 No 70040 *Clive of India* arrives at Peterborough North with a down Kings Cross-Cleethorpes train on 23 July 1962. *Dennis C. Ovenden*

134
BR '9F' 2-10-0 No 92040 deputises for a Southern Region Type 3 diesel on the Uddingston-Holborough cement tanker empties. Approaching Knebworth, 25 May 1963. *D. L. Percival*

135
Almost at the end of steam working at Kings Cross, 'A3' 4-6-2 No 60061 *Pretty Polly* departs with the 18.26 to Doncaster and Hull on 12 June 1963. *D. L. Percival*

136
The last ever 'A4' to leave Kings Cross. No 60009 *Union of South Africa* with the SLS/RCTS 'Jubilee Requiem' rail tour to Newcastle and back, 24 October 1964. *M. Pope*

Finale

In compiling this story the author has delved into records maintained by many friends to whom it is hoped the result will give pleasure and recall memories of countless hours of lineside observation in days long past. For those too young to remember the development of the Gresley Pacifics; the exciting days of the streamlined trains; the devotion to duty by countless enginemen and many more notable events of East Coast history, maybe they will obtain insight into the underlying reasons for our enthusiasm.

Over the 40 year span of this book successive changes in motive power, track and signalling alterations, closure of branch lines, stations and marshalling yards had altered the scene dramatically. Kings Cross station retains its original outline but internally is barely recognisable. In 1939 14 different locomotive classes operated 182 weekday passenger train departures. By 1981 there were only four diesel and two EMU types handling 122 daily departures. At Finsbury Park in the morning peak between 7.57 and 10.05 only 38 up suburban trains called compared with 61 in 1939. The old atmosphere has vanished. Amid the unceasing drone of diesel engines it is virtually impossible to converse with drivers. At favourite lineside venues where once any particular train was easily recognised by its stock formation, roof-boards, engine or even the driver's face, one can no longer tell one train from another. Ultra intensive diagramming has made accurate monitoring impossible. Likewise one can no longer follow drivers through the turns in their links which, at Kings Cross, now consist of over 60 men on rosters changing day by day. The impulse to venture out on a frosty moonlight night to view the passage of 'Coronation's descendant has gone along with the characteristic beat of Gresley's engines mounting the grade to Potters Bar. All good things come to an end, 'tis said. Nowhere more true than for the ageing admirers of steam on the East Coast Route.